# Civil War
# Ghost Stories

# Civil War
# Ghost Stories

**ANGUS KONSTAM**

THUNDER BAY
P·R·E·S·S
San Diego, California

THUNDER BAY
P·R·E·S·S

Thunder Bay Press
An imprint of the Advantage Publishers Group
5880 Oberlin Drive, San Diego, CA 92121-4794
www.thunderbaybooks.com

ISBN-13: 978-1-59223-482-0
ISBN-10: 1-59223-482-8

Library of Congress Cataloging-in-Publication Data
available upon request.

Printed in China

1 2 3 4 5 09 08 07 06 05

Project Editor: Shaun Barrington
Designer: John Heritage
Picture Researcher: Jennifer Lord
Production: Malcolm Croft
Index: Steve Theobald
Reproduction: Anorax Imaging Ltd.

**Additional Captions**
**Page 1:** Union bugle with attachment points for lanyard.
**Page 2:** A moving portrait of a young Union infantryman in fatigue blouse and cap;
did his mother shorten the pants?
**Page 3:** A Union Eagle–style snare drum.
**Page 5:** Remains of a Sharps Model 1859 rifle (top). Brompton Mansion on
Marye's Heights, where Confederate artillery massed at the Battle of Fredericksburg,
December 1862 (bottom).

# Contents

# Introduction

*"I hold that the union of these States is perpetual . . . Physically speaking we cannot separate."*

ABRAHAM LINCOLN'S INAUGURAL ADDRESS

At four thirty on the morning of April 12, 1861, the gun captain in charge of a mortar on Johnston's Island in Charleston Harbor pulled a lanyard attached to his weapon's priming tube. The mortar fired, and its large shell traced a high arc through the early morning sky before bursting over Fort Sumter. It was the opening shot of a war that would claim the lives of over half a million Americans and divide a nation for four long, blood-soaked years. The war would be fought from Pennsylvania to Florida and from Maryland to New Mexico, while combatant warships of both North and South would range the

*Below: The Maryland Memorial on the battlefield of Antietam, dedicated to the soldiers from the state who fought on both sides during the conflict. For Marylanders the Civil War truly was an internecine conflict.*

waters of the globe in search of American merchant ships or enemy raiders. Until the mid-twentieth century, it would be the largest war ever fought by the American people, and during its course, it would change the lives of every American. It was also the most traumatic event that many of the participants ever experienced: they watched their friends torn apart by artillery shot as they marched beside them, or they watched helplessly as brothers succumbed to sickness or disease. The technology of battle meant that soldiers of both sides were armed with relatively modern rifled muskets, or even repeating weapons, while rifled artillery pieces or large smoothbore guns demonstrated a power to kill and maim that the untrained volunteer soldiers in both armies found horrifying. A Union general summed up the horror of battle in his

description of a Confederate assault at the Battle of Gaines's Mill (1862):

Dashing across the intervening plain, floundering in the swamps, and struggling against the tangled brushwood, brigade after brigade seemed to melt away before the concentrated fire of our artillery and infantry; yet others pressed on, followed by supports as dashing and brave as their predecessors, despite their heavy losses and the disheartening effect of having to clamber over many of their disabled and dead, and to meet their surviving comrades rushing back in great disorder from the deadly contest.

Most battles in the war were won or lost through a massed infantry charge against an enemy who was waiting for them, with artillery and muskets sweeping the ground over which the troops approached the defender's line. Lee's attacks at Mechanicsville, Gaines's Mill, and Malvern Hill were matched in their slaughter only by similar Union attacks at Manassas, Antietam, and Fredericksburg.

Men who had never commanded troops before found themselves in charge of whole regiments, while junior officers of the peacetime army were catapulted into command of divisions, corps, or armies.

Inevitably, the learning curve was a steep one, particularly for the Union, whose commanders seemed to be chosen for their incompetence rather than their professionalism. As a result, thousands of lives were lost in needlessly costly frontal assaults, or wasted through poor camp hygiene or the lack of proper clothing. As the gifted Confederate General Daniel H. Hill said during the fighting around Richmond in the summer of 1862:

*Right: Sergeant Dore of the 7th New York State Militia regiment is typical of the soldiers of both sides who volunteered at the start of the conflict. They were soon exposed to the full horrors of the war on the battlefields of Manassas, Shiloh, and Gaines's Mill.*

*We were lavish of blood in those days, and it was thought to be a great thing to charge a battery of artillery or an earth-work lined with infantry.*

Although standards of military competence improved as the generals gained more experience or the more incompetent commanders were removed from active duty, mistakes were still made. Prime examples were Lee's launch of Pickett's Charge at Gettysburg in 1863, or Grant's decision to launch a massed frontal attack on the Confederate entrenchments at Cold Harbor a year later. The aftermath of these slaughters was devastating for the survivors of the

fighting, as smashed bodies lay amid the detritus of war, while the cries of the wounded and the dying clamored for help, for water, or for comfort. In some places such as the "Bloody Lane" at Antietam or the "Bloody Angle" at Spotsylvania, it was said you could literally walk for dozens of yards on the bodies without having to touch the blood-soaked ground. It is hardly surprising that the

*Below: A trio of Confederate soldiers from a Georgia Volunteer regiment photographed in early 1862, shortly before the bloodletting of the Seven Days Battles. Two of the three soldiers in the photograph were killed before the end of the summer's fighting.*

images of such scenes would have remained with the participants throughout their lives, and the horrors they saw haunted their memories. It has also been claimed that the same trauma experienced by the fallen soldiers in their moment of death also lingered long after the fighting was over, the sheer power of these terrible minutes causing the spirits of the dead to remain behind on the field of battle.

*Below: A Sunday Mass held for Catholic soldiers in the camp of the 69th New York State Militia regiment during the summer of 1862. Many soldiers turned to religion for solace or in search of an explanation for the horrors they witnessed.*

Now, most people claim to take ghost stories with "a grain of salt," consigning such tales to the same category as UFO sightings, the more outlandish conspiracy theories and stories of strange mythological creatures in the same category. It is extremely easy to be skeptical, to dismiss such stories as mere fantasies.

However, this book will show that accounts of these inexplicable happenings are not uncommon, and the shared experience of the horrors of war means that often very similar forms of haunting have been associated with battlefields as far apart as Shiloh in Tennessee and Gettysburg in Pennsylvania.

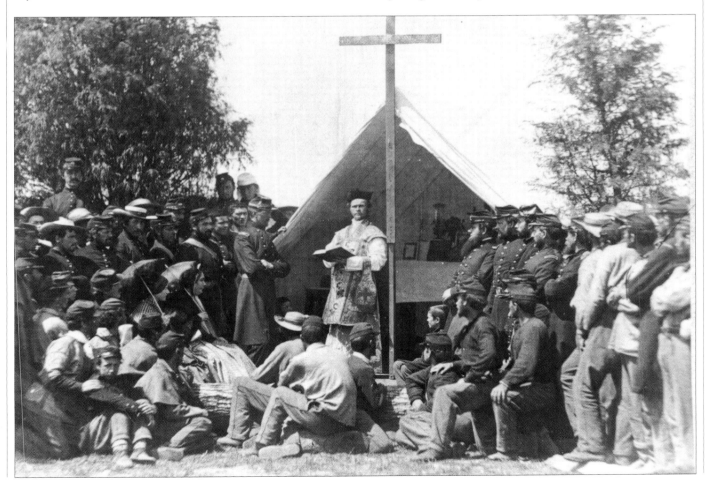

*Opposite: This studio portrait of a well-armed Union cavalryman is typical of the somewhat staid photographs that thousands of men posed for before they marched off to war. In thousands of cases, this photograph became the sole memento of them left behind for their grieving families.*

The most common form of ghostly occurrence is the kind ghost experts call a "residual haunting." These are cases where an apparition is seen performing the same things over and over again, or where the same mysterious sounds are heard in the same place on numerous occasions. These "residual hauntings" also seem to take place at the same time of the day, month, or year, as if repeating the sequence of events for all eternity.

In many of these cases, the witnesses have said that it seems to them that the ghost takes no notice of their human presence. The result is something akin to a taped film or soundtrack playing a loop again and again. Ghost researcher Dave Juliano offers the following account of the phenomenon:

Video and audio tapes capture sounds and images on a film of special material that has been oxidized or rusted. Certain building materials, such as slate used in older castles and stone structures and iron nails used in many older buildings, have properties similar to that of the tapes. When a traumatic event occurs or a time of heightened emotions, these materials record the event for future playback. Everything is made up of energy and energy cannot be destroyed. The materials store the energy created by these traumatic events and plays them back at a later time. The Tower of London's ghost of Anne Boleyn and the Brown Lady of Raynham Hall are two famous examples of residual haunting. We are not sure what causes the playback of the events, which still remains a mystery. Is it the right weather conditions, the witness's energy or sensitivity or some type of energy release? That is the question that we as researchers are trying to answer.

*Above: The Confederate horseman captured in this somewhat haunting portrait is armed with a single-shot carbine, which was no match for the modern breech-loading Sharps carbine carried by his Union counterpart on the opposite page.*

As the spirits involved in this type of haunting seem to ignore the presence of modern-day observers, the events themselves seem to have not appeared threatening to those who claim to have experienced them. The ghosts are benign, concerned with the reenactment of certain events rather than threatening the living. However, other reports of Civil War haunting are far more alarming, where the image seen by witnesses interacts with the observers and even seems to want to harm them in some way, or at least drive them away from a certain area. Others appear to want to draw attention to themselves, as if to attract the living to the injustices or injuries they suffered in the past, or to guide witnesses to a particular location relating to their death. In these pages, readers will discover both kinds of ghostly encounters: the harmless "residual" kind and those where the ghosts require something of the living.

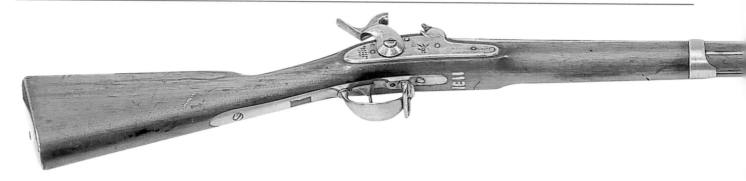

Whether you believe these stories is up to you. I am a bona fide and widely published historian, with no previous background in the supernatural. Indeed, were it not for my Scottish roots, I would willingly dismiss such tales as mere "hokum." I have a background where folklore involving

*Below: A Union ambulance unit removing the wounded from a battlefield during McClellan's Peninsular Campaign of 1862. Even the well-equipped Army of the Potomac was hard pressed to deal with the large number of casualties produced by full-scale battles, and many seriously wounded soldiers died before they could be treated.*

the supernatural formed part of my traditional Scottish upbringing, which was somewhat at odds with a later professional training as an archaeologist and historian, where I was taught to doubt all but the most tangible of evidence and to use scientific approaches to answer questions about the past. During research on books covering the history of the Civil War, I kept coming across stories that played on my Celtic roots rather than my academic training. During the course of my writing career, I have visited the battlefields mentioned in this book. Standing on the now peaceful woods or fields of places like Manassas, Chancellors-

*Above: Union Model 1842 smoothbore musket. A great variety of long arms was used by both sides in the conflict. For the Confederate soldier in particular there was little uiformity. He may well have picked up his own firearm and marched off to war. The remains of such weapons littered the battlefields.*

ville, Antietam, Gettysburg, or Chickamauga, it is all too easy to imagine what happened during those turbulent days during the Civil War and also to imagine that the spirits of those who fought and died there might not be too far away. The amalgam of these influences are reflected in this book, where I have tried to present the facts as far as they are known and have been able to dismiss many of these stories as having no foundation. However, I have also come across others that are far harder to dismiss, either because they have been well documented or because the supernatural events have been witnessed by several people, including

reliable nonpartisan witnesses. The conclusion seems to be that, while a rational explanation for some of these stories can be found if one digs deeply enough, others defy such comforting explanation. By adopting this fairly skeptical approach, the ghost stories that withstand scrutiny become even more intriguing.

The following example shows why skepticism can sometimes be the best policy when it comes to ghost stories. One of the most commonly heard ghost tales relating to the Battle of Gettysburg in July 1863 centers around the appearance of a mysterious rider who materialized on the eve of battle on the roads leading towards Gettysburg somewhere near Little Round Top. The standard version of the tale goes something like this:

On July 2, 1863, the forward units of General George Meade's Army of the Potomac were deployed on Cemetery Hill and Cemetery Ridge near the Pennsylvania crossroads town of Gettysburg. General Lee's Army of Northern Virginia fought better the previous day, but most of his army still had not reached the battlefield. Reinforcements from both sides arrived in the area during the day, and by late afternoon Lee ordered General James Longstreet to launch an attack on the Union left flank in the vicinity of Little Round Top. As other Union columns were marching toward the sound of the guns, the defenders in the salient in front of the hill were forced back by Longstreet's men, and it became clear that, unless reinforcements were rushed to the battle, the Confederates would capture both Round Top, Devil's Den, and Little Round Top. With these territories in Confederate hands, the flank of the Union position along Cemetery Ridge would be turned, and Meade's strong defensive position would become untenable. It became a race, with Longstreet throwing General John Hood's division around the flank of the Union defenders and heading straight for the two small hills, while Meade sent runners back to find troops who could fill the gap. It was then that the phantom horseman appeared.

On the Taneytown Road, General Sykes's V Corps was marching north when it received the order to swing to the left and to deploy on the two hills in support of Major General Daniel Sickles's hard-pressed III Corps. At around four in the afternoon, the first two divisions deployed into position, but Sykes's 3rd Division was still far to the rear. In the leading ranks of its 3rd Brigade was Colonel Joshua Chamberlain's 20th Maine Volunteers, a unit that would more than distinguish itself in the fighting later that evening. Chamberlain noticed that there seemed to be some confusion, since staff officers seemed to be riding up and down the column, as if unsure where exactly to deploy the troops. At that crucial moment, Chamberlain spotted another rider cantering past, mounted on a superb-looking horse. The rider moved past the head of the column, then disappeared out of sight further up the road. A staff officer took the figure to be the former commander of the army, General George McClellan, and told each colonel in turn, "General McClellan is in command again, and he's riding up ahead of us on the road." According to the story, in Chamberlain's words, "men waved their hats, cheered until they were hoarse, and wild with excitement, followed the figure on horseback. Although weary, they marched with the miraculous enthusiasm believing that their beloved general had returned to lead them into battle."

The figure of the rider reached a little further on the column and was standing beside the road motioning for the men to turn off and follow him. It was then that they noticed his uniform. Although it was blue like the rest of the troops, it seemed to be more colorful and cut slightly better. Even more incongruously, McClellan (or whoever the man was) was wearing a tricorne hat, something that had fallen from military fashion seventy years before. Then the horseman revealed its face. According to Chamberlain, a gasp went up, followed by a growing murmur from the men.

It was no other than George Washington. The American army's first Commander-in-Chief had apparently returned to the fray to lead the Union army into battle. The men began cheering, and invigorated by the ghostly apparition, they headed into battle eager to meet the enemy. The figure then rode off into the trees and was never seen again. What followed is well-recorded history. The 20th Maine formed part of the line protecting the two hills, and their spirited defense of Little Round Top helped change the tide of the battle. However, the story doesn't quite end there.

At a crucial moment in the fighting for Little Round Top, Chamberlain launched a bayonet charge down the hill to drive off the last of the Confederate attackers. According to the story, the horseman suddenly materialized again, standing in front of the regiment and waving his sword.

Inspired by the vision, the 20th Maine charged down the hill and routed the Alabama troops in their path. Although other versions of the story have also appeared, this version is the most common.

There is only one real problem with the story. It never happened. In his highly detailed report of the battle, Chamberlain wrote:

Somewhere near 4 pm a sharp cannonade, at some distance to our left and front, was the signal for a sudden and rapid movement of our whole division in the direction of this firing, which grew warmer as we approached. Passing an open field in the hollow ground in which some of our batteries were going into position, our brigade reached the skirt of a piece of woods, in the farther edge of which there was a heavy musketry fire, and when about to go forward into line we received from Colonel Vincent, commanding the brigade, orders to move to the left at the double-quick, when we took a farm road crossing Plum Run in order to gain a rugged mountain spur called Granite Spur, or Little Round Top.

In other words, the regiment was directed into place by the Brigade commander, not by the ghost of George Washington. Speaking of the bayonet charge, he told of the pressure the regiment was under, and how he decided to take the initiative before his regiment was overwhelmed:

It was imperative to strike before we were struck by this overwhelming force in a hand-to-hand fight, which we could not probably have withstood or survived. At that crisis, I ordered the bayonet. The word was enough. It ran like fire along the line, from man to man, and rose into a shout, with which they sprang forward upon the enemy, now not 30 yards away. The effect was surprising; many of the enemy's first line threw down their arms and surrendered. An officer fired his pistol at my head with one hand, while he handed me his sword with the other. Holding fast by our right, and swinging forward our left, we made an extended "right wheel," before which the enemy's second line broke and fell back, fighting from tree to tree, many being captured, until we had swept the valley and cleared the front of nearly our entire brigade.

The inspiration to charge came not from the equestrian ghost of George Washington but from Chamberlain himself. We know this because of Chamberlain's original report as well as copies of his personal correspondence after the battle.

It is difficult to find out exactly where the ghost story began, but it is pretty certain that it did not originate on the battlefield on the afternoon of July 2, 1863. The story has been repeated by several leading ghost-story writers, and one book even claims that there was an official War Department investigation into the incident, where a Colonel Pittenger looked into the ghostly sighting and even interviewed several senior commanders who saw the apparition, including General Oliver Howard. Unfortunately, extensive archival research failed to produce any evidence of an investigation or even of a staff officer in the

**Above:** *Confederate casualties in one of the trenches outside Petersburg, Virginia, photographed on April 2, 1865, when the remnants of Lee's battered army were forced to abandon the city and retreat toward Appomatox for the final acts of the war. These men were a week away from the surrender—and salvation.*

War Department named Pittenger. Even more revealing, Oliver Howard's *Autobiography of Oliver Otis Howard* (1907) made no mention of seeing a ghost that day or of being interviewed by a secret War Department committee. While it would be all too easy to repeat this story—a narration that has gained respectability through repeated airing—as fact, to do so would be to go against all the principles of historical research.

One day, someone might come up with hard evidence that something did indeed happen that day and that the story was subsequently covered up by the army, but until they do, the whole phantom horseman story has to be filed under fiction.

However, as you shall discover, there are plenty more Civil War ghost stories that are not so easily dismantled and dismissed, where there is more evidence to support their telling.

# ANTEBELLUM GHOSTS

THE FIRST PREREQUISITE for ghostly phenomena seems to be the passage of time. While the United States may not be a very old country, its history, which includes the establishment of the original colonies, the War of Independence, and the Civil War, is sufficient on this point. Where the United States can likely claim a terrible superiority to some other nations is in the second prerequisite: suffering on home soil. And the awful loss of life, in battle and from disease, in the Civil War itself was predicated on another kind of suffering: slavery.

If, as some theorists of the supernatural suggest, ghostly phenomena are expressions of untimely human loss or unwarranted suffering, then it is not surprising that antebellum ghosts abound, some in the old plantations of the South, some who never made it to freedom.

*Left: It is difficult to imagine the sun-kissed Kingsley Plantation near Jacksonville, Florida, having any association with ghosts, but the house and its grounds have long been associated with a grisly ghost story from the days of slavery.*

# Ghosts of the Plantation

*"The beautiful, proud Sunny South, with its masters and mistresses, was bowed beneath the sin brought about by slavery."*

ANNIE L. BURTON, MEMORIES OF CHILDHOOD DAYS, *1909*

Given the traumatic human condition of slavery and the often harsh life on the plantation, it is surprising that so few ghost stories bear more than the most cursory examination. Many appear to be little more than copycat tales, where stories associated with one plantation have been adapted for use on another. One reason for these oft-repeated tales is tourism, the lifeblood of America's historic house, where it is perhaps unsurprising that every historic site is expected to harbor a ghost or two. This makes the few original tales that remain all the more intriguing. Although the ghost stories associated with these antebellum mansions are potentially numerous enough to fill a book in their own right, we have selected a small sample of the most interesting of these tales, which will serve as a useful precursor to our study of Civil War ghosts. In addition, a few of those where the stories seem to have been embellished or concocted are also fascinating in their own right, at least as far as they demonstrate the need people have to associated a ghostly tale with their property. Finally, one additional tale has been included that, although not related to any plantation houses, helps complete the survey of ghost stories associated with slavery and suffering in antebellum America.

While tobacco plantations existed in Virginia and North Carolina since the mid-seventeenth century, it was not until the first decades of the eighteenth century that the

*Opposite: The Sherwood Forest Plantation in Charles City, Virginia, was once home to President Tyler and, like the neighboring Shirley Plantation, the historic home is supposed to have its own antebellum ghost.*

*Left: The harsh treatment meted out to African American slaves during the antebellum era has produced its own crop of ghost stories that reflect the miseries of institutional slavery and the desire for freedom.*

plantation system of agriculture really took hold in the southern of Britain's North American colonies. The development of rice as a cash crop transformed the agricultural landscape of Georgia and South Carolina, and by 1750 plantation agriculture based on the use of African American slaves had come to dominate the economy of the South. Rice and indigo were increasingly important exports during the colonial period, but the American Revolution severely damaged the indigo market with Britain, while rice exports took decades to return to their pre-Revolutionary levels. During the early nineteenth century, the importance of rice and tobacco became overshadowed by the growth of the cultivation of cotton, a cash crop that required an even greater number of slaves to harvest. During the decades before the Civil War, the production of "King Cotton" extended from the coastal states into Alabama, Mississippi, and Louisiana. This meant that large plantation houses and their attendant slave quarters could be found from Virginia to Florida and from the Carolinas to beyond the Mississippi River. Although many plantation houses were destroyed during the Civil War, dozens still remain today as reminders of an old way of life, where the genteel ways of the Old Southern planter aristocracy existed side by side with the soul-destroying torment of involuntary servitude.

The Kingsley Plantation on Fort George Island near Jacksonville, Florida, is reputedly the home of a slave ghost. The island itself was once home to a group of Timucuan Indians, but they seemed to have sold or

ceded their land to the British authorities shortly after the land was transferred from Spanish ownership. A rice and indigo plantation was established there by a J. Tucker in 1767, and it remained in operation after Florida was ceded back to Spain in 1783. In 1791, another planter, John McQueen, took over, encouraged by a Spanish land grant, until debt forced him to sell his property. By 1804 Kingsley was owned by John McIntosh, who soon became the wealthiest planter in Florida, owning 170 slaves. By this time, sea cotton had been established as the principal crop on the plantation. The War of 1812 led to an invasion of Spanish Florida by the U.S. Army, a preemptive strike to avoid Florida falling into British hands. The threat of war forced McIntosh to sell the property to a fellow Scot, Zephaniah Kingsley, who lived on the plantation with his freed-slave mistress and then wife, Anna Madgigine Jai. The Kingsley plantation remained in their hands through the transfer of Florida to the United States in 1821, but the change of government meant that more repressive slavery laws came into effect. Kingsley had been a largely benevolent slave owner, a stance encouraged by Spanish law. He eventually sold his holdings and his slaves, and he and his wife moved to Haiti. Today, the plantation is owned and operated by the National Park Service, and visitors can tour the house and grounds and examine the remains of some twenty-five slave cabins. They might also catch a glimpse of a ghost.

Reputedly the plantation is haunted by the ghost of a former slave nicknamed "Old Red Eyes." He worked on the plantation after it was sold by the Kingsleys and abducted two young slave girls from the plantation during the 1840s. He tied them up and took them to a hideout in the woods on Fort George Island. After raping the girls, he tortured and killed them, death no doubt coming as a blessed release after the agonies inflicted upon them by the man.

An investigation was held into the disappearance of the two young girls, and eventually "Old Red Eyes" was identified as their abductor and murderer. He was tried for his crimes, then hanged from one of the trees lin-

ing the plantation. The story goes that the cries of his child victims can still be heard on some nights, while others report seeing two red, evil eyes watching them from the darkness, sightings that earned the former slave his nickname and have come to be closely associated with the tale of the sadistic murderer from the pre–Civil War era. Even more disconcerting, drivers passing through the area have apparently reported seeing two red eyes staring at them in their rearview mirror, although when they turned around, there was nothing there.

Another ghost has also been associated with the plantation, that of a woman dressed in white, who has been seen sitting on the porch of the main plantation building. Some claim this is the ghost of the former slave Anna Jai Kingsley, returning from time to time to watch over her husband's plantation. It has even been claimed that the woman in white has been photographed, although no convincing evidence of her manifestation has ever been produced.

One of the grandest surviving plantation houses is that of the Shirley Plantation in Charles City, Virginia, eighteen miles east of Richmond on scenic State Route 5. Established in 1613, Shirley is the oldest plantation in Virginia and has remained in the hands of the same family and its descendants since the 1640s. Anne Hill Carter, the mother of the legendary Confederate general Robert E. Lee, was raised in Shirley's plantation house, and it was there that she married her husband Henry "Light Horse Harry" Lee. The mansion was built between 1723 and 1738, with very few modifications made over the centuries. Today visitors come to admire its fine interiors, impressive "flying" staircase, and the many family portraits that line the walls of the mansion. One of these paintings features a Hill family member known as "Aunt Pratt." Her full name was actually Martha Hill, the daughter of Edward Hill III. She married an Englishman and returned with him to Britain where she died in 1752. Traditionally, her portrait hung on the wall of the main-floor bedroom, but the story goes that when the painting was moved during a renovation in 1858, the owners were plagued by loud and mysterious nocturnal activities coming from the attic where the painting was stored. Most notably, this took the form of the sound of rocking. When the painting was rehung on the second or third floors, the sounds continued in the new location. Although nothing was ever seen, the owners became convinced that the ghostly sounds were associated with the painting, which they assumed was haunted. When Martha's portrait was returned to her original position, the ghostly sounds ceased.

While it is easy to dismiss this story as mere superstition, the current occupants of the house are determined never to move the painting from its position. They did so once in 1974, when the painting was loaned out for an exhibition. Curators and visitors alike reported they saw the painting move, and the vibration it caused apparently caused enough disturbance to make the other paintings alongside it appear to move too. It was hurriedly returned to Shirley Plantation.

The story is similar to that of the "Gray Lady" who is said to haunt the neighboring plantation of Sherwood Forest, once the home of President John Tyler. She has been heard to knock on the walls and door of the "Gray Room" in the mansion and has done so since before the Civil War. According to the story, the ghost is that of a former governess who served the Tyler family and who is said to have unsuccessfully nursed an ailing child in the room.

The Myrtles Plantation near St. Francisville, Louisiana, was built by a General David Bradford in 1796. His plantation home is now a guest house, where a major attraction for guests is the association the Myrtles has with several ghosts. According to the stories, no less than ten murders were committed in the house, including those involving a slave girl named Chloe in the 1850s. When she was caught eavesdropping by the antebellum owner's son, Judge Clarke Woodruff, the owner cut off his slave's ear. In retaliation, Chloe poisoned a children's birthday cake with oleander, killing her attacker's two young daughters. Chloe's actions were uncovered, and she was hanged for the murder. The ghosts of the two young girls are supposed to haunt the veranda of the plantation house,

*Left: John Tyler (1790–1862), the ninth U.S. President was also the first vice president to ascend to the presidency following the death of William Henry Harrison in 1841. His home is said to be haunted by the ghost of the "Gray Lady."*

*Right: Tyler's plantation home was first built in 1720, and when he purchased the property from his cousin in 1842, he renamed the plantation "Sherwood Forest" as a proud reference to his reputation as something of a political outlaw.*

innocently playing while their murderess bakes her poisoned cake. The ghost of Chloe is also reported to stalk the grounds, and a photograph of the slave girl has even been produced as evidence of her spiritual existence. Other ghosts have been associated with the nearby slave's graveyard.

Unfortunately, some ghost hunters have cast doubt on this splendidly melodramatic story. First, the slave records associated with the plantation apparently make no mention of the slave girl Chloe, while the two girls are recorded as having died of yellow fever—and not at the same time but almost a year apart—in 1824. In addition, the Judge's son James also succumbed during the same period, a time when a yellow fever epidemic was known to have been sweeping Louisiana. Further, only one murder can be accurately attributed to the plantation: that of William Drew Winter, a former plantation manager who married into the owning family and was shot on the veranda of the Myrtles Plantation in 1871.

While many remain skeptical of these ghost stories, one researcher states that the Myrtles Plantation is indeed a legitimate place

to investigate, as the plantation has such a long and colorful history, regardless of the truth of the ghost stories. However, he also added that there is a strong possibility that at least some of the phenomena there are not associated with the stories that have become so overpublicized by the plantation's owners. Another goes even further, claiming that no ghost stories were ever associated with the plantation until it was bought by a Californian couple in the 1970s. Some also report that tour guides on the plantation now seem reluctant to mention many of these ghost stories because of the concerns of the State of Louisiana's Historical Society that they were generated to encourage tourism and have little basis in historical fact. Other visitors are convinced they have experienced paranormal activity on the Myrtles Plantation and go away certain they have had a brush with the supernatural. Whatever the truth is, the plantation remains one of the most highly publicized haunted plantation sites in the Deep South.

Although not exactly a plantation house, the mansion at 1140 Royal Street in New Orleans's French Quarter has probably the most macabre link to antebellum slavery of any historic building in the South. During the 1830s, the new and imposing property was owned by a Dr. Louis Lalaurie and his wife Delphine, two of the most respected people in the city's French-Creole community. Although the exterior of the house was somewhat simple, its interiors were filled with the latest furniture from Paris: numerous chandeliers, expensive mirrors, and rich wall hangings. The doctor's dining table was one of the most exquisitely furnished in the city, and his social events were the talk of the town. The elegant Madame Lalaurie ran the household and supervised her extensive staff of house slaves. Eventually, rumors of mistreatment started to circulate around New Orleans. It was said that Madam Lalaurie chained her African American cook to the fireplace in the kitchen and that she was one of the lucky ones. A neighbor heard screaming and saw Madam Lalaurie chasing a small girl with a whip. The terrified slave child tried to escape by climbing onto the roof of the house, but she slipped and fell to her death. A few days later, the same neighbor noticed a small grave had appeared in a shaded corner of the Lalaurie's yard. His complaint led to an investigation by the authorities, and although the family slaves were briefly impounded, the Lalauries arranged for relatives to purchase them and then sell them back to their original owners. The rumors continued to spread. Others noticed that several of the Lalaurie household slaves simply disappeared, while others appeared terrified of their mistress.

Matters came to a head in April 1834. A fire broke out in the house, the reason for which has never been explained. The city's fire department was called and managed to extinguish the blaze, but in the process the men uncovered the Lalauries' secret. A fireman whose duty it was to inspect the house for any further traces of the fire reached the attic, where he found a true chamber of horrors. Ten or twelve slaves of both sexes were there, naked and either chained to the wall, strapped to a table, or locked in a cage. Parts of dismembered bodies were piled in buckets, while shelves contained whips, scourges, and other instruments of torture. While most of the slaves were dead, probably from smoke inhalation as much as anything else, a few remained alive, although brutally mutilated, and some were able to tell of their ordeal. According to the local newspaper, the *New Orleans Bee* in April 1834, some of these unfortunate souls had their stomachs opened and body parts ripped or sliced off. One woman even had her mouth filled with human excrement and then sewn shut.

Doctors were summoned, and the authorities were called. As they arrived, an angry mob was already gathering outside the house. Then the courtyard gates opened, and a carriage rushed out, driving through the crowd and away into the city. The Lalauries were never seen again. Rumor had it that they escaped to France, but their subsequent fate remains a mystery.

The first reports of haunting at 1140 Royal Street came soon afterwards. The house was bought in 1837, but the new owner only

*Above: The shako of a U.S. artilleryman dating from the first years of the Civil War. By 1862, impractical pieces of uniform like these were abandoned in favor of more practical and less conspicuous attire.*

**Right:** *Slave holding pens in Alexandria, Virginia, occupied by Union troops at the outbreak of war. The issue of slavery tore America apart in the mid-nineteenth century, making civil war all but inevitable.*

remained in residence for a few months, driven out by the nocturnal cries coming from the attic. He then leased parts of the house out but was unable to retain tenants for more than a few weeks. The house later became a school, then a private dwelling again, but throughout its subsequent history the property seemed dogged by reports of ghostly activity. One of these specters was that of a shackled black male slave who moved as if to attack the occupants before vanishing again. The screams from the attic continued, while other reports of the figure of a shrouded woman continued to circulate. Eventually, the house was turned into a bar, which cashed in on the property's notoriety by taking the name, The Haunted Saloon. Today, 1140 Royal Street has been turned into private apartments, but during this construction, workmen discovered a small graveyard in the house basement. Once the bodies were removed and buried properly, the hauntings seemed to stop.

The basic facts surrounding the sadistic Lalaurie couple do bear scrutiny, as the scandal did indeed take place, as did earlier reports of the mistreatment of slaves. However, the extent of the mutilations seem to have been (thankfully) exaggerated, and although the newspaper reported the finding of an operating table and even shackles in the attic, the scourges or cages seem to have been later embellishments to the story.

The popular version of the tale has Madame Lalaurie as the main culprit, and her husband was generally viewed as her unwilling accomplice. However, one persistent version names the doctor as the culprit, and the attic served as the place where he practiced his operating techniques on his unwilling house slaves, or conducted anatomical dissections on slaves who had died under his knife. Whatever the truth, it remains New Orleans's most dramatic and macabre tale from the antebellum era, and it is one of the city's best-known ghost stories.

# Ghost Train to Freedom

*"I looked at my hands to see if I was the same person now I was free . . . I never run my train off the track and I never lost a passenger."*

HARRIET TUBMAN

The Underground Railroad was an informal network established by antislavery activists in the northern states to assist fugitive slaves, concealing them from slave-hunters, bounty-hunters, and the authorities until the runaways reached the safety of the Canadian border. This clandestine support network was first established in the 1790s, and by the time of the Civil War, many thousands of fugitives were spirited away by abolitionist supporters. The success of the movement provided useful publicity for the abolitionist cause, and despite the best efforts of many, the Underground Railroad continued to develop, its activities reaching a peak during the decade preceding the outbreak of the war.

One of the best known clients of the Underground Railroad was Harriet Tubman (ca. 1820–1913), who escaped from slavery in Maryland in 1849 and then, as a "conductor," she made over fifteen trips back to the South to help others escape to freedom along the Railroad. Those who benefited from her efforts included her own siblings, who were brought out of Maryland and moved to Canada during the early 1850s. While many thousands of runaway slaves reached safety, others were not so fortunate. Some were caught and turned over to the authorities, while others were recaptured by slave-hunters. In some areas, lynch mobs and local vigilantes forced the runaways to pay the ultimate price for their quest for freedom. Many of the ghost stories emanating from the Underground Railroad are founded on incidents where the escape went horribly wrong or when those

providing the "stations" of refuge were uncovered and persecuted for their activities.

One of the most celebrated Railroad sites that has long had a ghostly association is Woodburn, the official residence of the governor of Delaware, near Dover. The land on which the house was built was purchased by landowner Charles Hillyard in 1784, and by 1798 Woodburn served as his family home. Following Hillyard's death in 1814, the house passed into the hands of his son-in-law Senator Bates, whose family sold the property in 1825. The new owner, Daniel Cowgill, passed the house on to his children, and it was later transferred to his granddaughter's husband, Edward Wilson, whose family retained the house into the early twentieth century.

Woodburn passed through several more hands before being purchased by the State of Delaware in 1965 and becoming the official residence of Governor Charles L. Terry. By that time, it had a widely spread reputation for being haunted.

According to legend, the ghost of the original owner, Charles Hillyard, still haunts his former mansion; he first appeared in front of a houseguest a year after his death. It is also claimed that if a glass of wine is left out downstairs during the night, by morning the glass will have been emptied. However, the wife of Governor (1973–1976) Sherman W. Tribbitt tested the theory and reported finding no trace of the wine-drinking ghost.

A second ghost associated with Woodburn was that of a small girl, rumored to appear in the grounds wearing a gingham dress and bonnet and carrying a candle.

*Opposite: The one-time runaway slave and ardent abolitionist Harriet Tubman helped pioneer the Underground Railroad and was responsible for spiriting something between seventy and three hundred runaway slaves to freedom in the decade before the Civil War. The hard facts about her activities are as difficult to pin down as ghost reports, partly from the postwar desire to believe in a prewar established network for slaves to escape. The Railroad was probably never really that organized, nor did it penetrate deep into the South.*

More importantly for our story, a large tulip poplar tree on the south lawn of Woodburn has long been associated with the ghost of a runaway slave. Although the ancient tree was removed in 1998, it had long been notable for its size and hollowed-out interior. Legend has it that during the 1850s, when Woodburn belonged to the Cowgill family, a runaway slave was being chased by a party of slave-hunters and took refuge in the grounds of Woodburn. On discovering the tree, he hid himself inside it, only to be tracked down by the dogs of his pursuers. The runaway slave was killed, and according to the story, his screams could still be heard occasionally. What weakens the story is that they have often been "heard" on Halloween, a date that would have meant little to either the slave or his pursuers and that owes its popularity to the "trick-or-treat" boom of the mid-twentieth century.

No ghostly screams have been reported since the remains of "Dead Man's Tree" were removed. Another version of the story claims that local slave-hunting vigilantes laid siege to Woodburn but were driven off by the Cowgill family and their servants. One attacker hid in the branches of the poplar but slipped from his perch. The story goes that his beard caught in the tree, and he died by accidental hanging. No evidence has been found to support either tale.

However, the location itself has a far more tangible link to the abolitionist movement. The Harriet Tubman Society records Woodburn as a station on the Underground Railroad during the 1840s and 1850s, when the property was owned by Daniel Cowgill. Tales persist of a secret tunnel running from a hidden room in the basement under the gardens to the nearby St. Jones River. From there, boats would transport runaway slaves to the Delaware River then north to safety. Though no trace of the tunnel has survived, it is probable that the Cowgills played their part in the Underground Railroad during those antebellum years.

A somewhat less wholesome site associated with an Underground Railroad ghost is found near Parsons, West Virginia: a tall rugged hill known as Darkish Knob. One of the many routes used by runaway slaves lay through the mountains of the western part of Virginia, an area where slave-owning was generally viewed with distaste and that seceded from Virginia in 1861 to form the new state of West Virginia. Parson lay astride one of these mountain routes, and a small cabin hidden in the woods and tumbled boulders beneath Darkish Knob was reputedly a secret station on the Underground Railroad where runaway slaves could find temporary refuge. According to legend, one such runaway was a young girl, mounted on a horse, who was being pursued by a group of slave-hunters. In the darkness she misread the directions to the cabin and followed the trail up Darkish Knob instead. As she approached the summit, her horse lost its footing and both horse and rider plunged down into the ravine of the Cheat River, where they were dashed on the rocks and killed. According to the tale, her pursuers were a mile behind and her heard a long scream that ended

abruptly. The story goes that, on the anniversary of her death, the girl's spirit returns to the cliff top, then cries in fear for several minutes before it lets out her long, final scream. Like so many ghost stories, the tale is full of ambiguities, and no hard evidence for either the cabin or the slave girl has ever been forthcoming. While it makes a good ghost story, the tale could be a concocted one, or else an apocryphal tale based on some other event and retold to serve the needs of a new audience.

A similar tale centers on another cabin used as a Railroad resting place, this time outside Fairmont, West Virginia, close to the Buckhannon River and some thirty miles northwest of the cabin beneath Darkish Knob. A group of runaway slaves were hidden in the cabin when it was surrounded and attacked by a group of local vigilantes. According to the local West Virginia legend, the attackers killed the slaves and cut off their heads, leaving the bodies where they lay and taking the heads to the nearby river and throwing them in. The owner of the cabin buried the headless victims in his family plot, but since then ghostly lights have been seen coming from the cabin and its immediate vicinity. Naturally, this was explained away as the ghosts of the dead searching for their missing heads. Once again, there seems to be no historic evidence to support such an event, but the persistence of the legend suggests that this ghastly deed or something like it linked to the Underground Railroad may well have taken place near Fairmont in the decade before the Civil War began.

An equally disturbing ghostly tale emerged from Millington, New Jersey, an important "switch" area on the Underground Railroad where runaway slaves could either be led northwest toward the Canadian border or northeast toward New York and New England. Today a monument celebrates the local activities of the Underground Railroad, although less tangible reminders have also been reported. Several engineers working on the railroad tracks that curve around Millington reported seeing the figures of a tall black man standing on the tracks near where they cross the Passaic River. The figure was described as wearing a large cloak or robe. A similar figure was seen by local residents standing on the old rail bridge that goes over the river; one of these locals added

the detail that the man carried a wooden staff and had red, bloodshot eyes. According to local legend, a group of Millington residents held a séance that conjured up the ghost of the man, who gave his name as Yagoo, a freed-slave conductor on the Underground Railroad who reportedly led groups over the railroad bridge under cover of darkness so they could reach a safe haven in Millington.

During the first decade of the nineteenth century, several residents of nearby Oaks Road claimed they were repeatedly visited by ghostly apparitions: the figures of runaway slaves walking east from the railroad bridge towards the center of the town. Since then, the ghost of Yagoo has occasionally been sighted, but no more large-scale sightings were reported.

*Below: Woodburn, Delaware, the official residence of the state governor, was built in 1798 and has been associated with ghosts since 1815. It is claimed that during the 1850s, the house was used as a station on the Underground Railroad.*

Two more haunted sites are found in Washington, D.C., where two historic houses became closely associated with the Underground Railroad and the ghosts of those runaway slaves who passed through their portals. On the corner of New York Avenue and Eighteenth Street NW stands the Octagon House, once the home of President Madison while the White House was being rebuilt after it was burned by the British in 1814. Madison's wife Dolley is supposed to have so loved the place that she returns there to dance and smell the lilacs.

Although Dolley Madison has long been associated with the house, as have the ghostly daughters of the building's first owner, the most commonly reported sightings are of former slaves. Legend has it that tunnels led into the basement of the house from the Potomac River, and these were used to spirit runaway slaves into the heart of the city without risk of being detected. The voices of these former slaves have reportedly been heard in the house, while the story of another slave who was killed then buried in a wall has been used to explain other strange noises: sobs and the sound of knocking on a wall. While all these

ghostly tales may have some explanation, no trace of the tunnel system has ever been found, making it unlikely that the Octagon House played a major part in the Underground Railroad. The current owners of the building, the American Institute of Architecture, have never claimed any ghostly happenings in the house at all, and since they have been in residence for just over a century, it seems that if any ghosts were once associated with the house, then they no longer trouble the residents of the building.

In Georgetown, Halcyon House was built by the first secretary of the Navy, Benjamin Stoddert, in 1783. The modest building forming the heart of his Pretty Prospect Estate was added to over the years until it bore little resemblance to its original form. It now stands on the junction of Prospect and Thirty-fourth Street NW, although its front door still faces the river, reflecting Stoddert's maritime interests.

During the decade before the Civil War, the house became an important staging post, or station, in the Underground Railroad. Built close to the Potomac River, the house provided shelter for runaway slaves who were able to swim across from the Virginia riverbank. A drainage tunnel connected the house to the riverbank, which provided easy access for the runaways, so that the other inhabitants of Georgetown were unaware that Halcyon House was a safe haven for slaves. The river crossing was hazardous, especially in winter, and many runaway slaves failed to reach the far shore and the safety of Halcyon House. Others were reputedly so traumatized by their exertions that they expired from fatigue or exposure in the basement of the house itself.

Over the years, there have been numerous reports that the sound of moaning or people moving around has been heard coming from the basement, and this has been credited to the ghosts of ailing or dying runaway slaves, expiring at their first station on the road to freedom.

It was reported that in the first decade of the twentieth century, the family who owned the house decided to block up the tunnel, as rats were entering the house from the river. The builder who set about the task was alarmed when he heard cries and weeping coming from the tunnel and the basement around him. After he bricked up the tunnel entrance, he began plastering over the new wall, but he froze when he heard a sudden scream come from the far side of the newly blocked tunnel. He fled, leaving his tools where they lay, and never returned.

These supposed slave ghosts were not the only supernatural association with Halcyon House. In the 1930s, it was sold to an Albert Clemons, who convinced himself that if he

kept adding to the house, he would never die. Consequently, he added pointless walls and a staircase leading nowhere, as well as additional rooms and wings to the house. Despite all his best efforts, he duly died of a fairly ripe old age. His ghost is still reported to roam the corridors of the house, as is that of a mysterious, faceless woman.

Incidentally, just a few blocks away on Wisconsin Avenue, patrons of a bar called Mr. Henry's have reputedly heard the ghosts of slaves singing and dancing. The slave quarters of an estate stood on the site during the first decades of the nineteenth century.

It seems ironic that the ghosts of these slaves seemed to have been enjoying a far more pleasant eternity than those who made their courageous break for freedom and tragically died in the attempt.

*Right: During the early nineteenth century, the Octagon House was owned by Colonel George Tayloe, an old friend of George Washington. The ghosts of two of his daughters are said to haunt the property.*

# John Brown's Body—and Spirit

*"Here, before God, in the presence of these witnesses,
I consecrate my life to the destruction of slavery . . ."*

JOHN BROWN, 1837

On the night of Sunday, October 16, 1859 the militant abolitionist John Brown crossed the Potomac River from the northern Maryland bank and entered the town of Harpers Ferry, Virginia. He was accompanied by a twenty-one-man "Army of Liberation," including two of his sons and four African Americans, and his men drove a wagon containing enough muskets and homemade spears to arm 1,350 men. His plan was to seize the military arsenal and the U.S. Army Musket Factory in the town and then incite a general slave rebellion in the Shenandoah Valley.

Armed with the weapons brought by Brown and those in the arsenal, the slaves could then extend the rebellion through the rest of the slave states of America. Ironically, the first man who was gunned down by Brown and his men was Shephard Hayward, a free African American, the porter at the local train station. The abolitionists quickly took over the arsenal and rounded up several hostages, then established themselves in the armory's engine house, which was turned into a miniature fort. By the following morning, angry citizens had thrown a cordon around the engine

*Opposite: The quiet West Virginia town of Harpers Ferry became a battleground in October 1859 when John Brown and his gang blockaded themselves into the engine house in the bottom right of this picture, while residents laid siege to the building from the safety of neighboring houses.*

*Inset: The radical abolitionist John Brown (1800–1859) was already wanted for murder when he arrived in Harpers Ferry, where he hoped to lead Virginia's slaves into bloody revolt against their masters.*

*Left: Harpers Ferry occupied a key strategic location at the confluence of the Potomac and Shenandoah rivers, with rail and road bridges linking Virginia to Maryland. It was also the site of a major weapons factory. Brown hoped to use the town as a base and supply-center for his armed slave insurrection.*

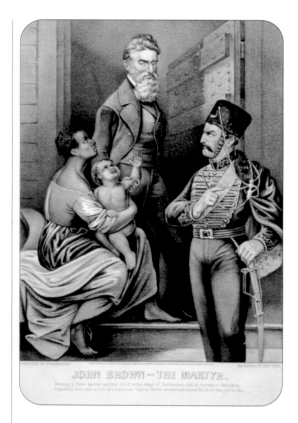

JOHN BROWN—THE MARTYR.

Left: *"John Brown the mar-tyr" prepares to kiss the child of a slave woman en route to the scaffold. Martyrs have a tendency to bring death to others in their wakes, and Brown, the justness of his cause notwithstanding, is no exception to the grim rule.*

house, and their anger increased when Brown's men shot and killed the town mayor, Colonel Fontaine Beckham. A siege began, with fire being exchanged by both sides. That morning, both of Brown's sons were mortally wounded, and the growing despair of the abolitionists must have reached a peak during the early hours of October 18, when a contingent of U.S. Marines arrived, led by Lieutenant Colonel Robert E. Lee and his deputy, Lieutenant "Jeb" Stuart. The two Virginian officers called on Brown to surrender, and after he refused, Lee ordered his marines to storm the engine house. Within minutes it was all over, and, while only one marine was killed and another wounded, the entire abolitionist force was killed, wounded, or captured.

John Brown and his surviving band were tried and convicted of treason, incitement of rebellion, and murder. The verdict was never in doubt: Brown had already murdered slave-owners in Kansas, and despite any abolitionist sentiments in the free states, there was no doubt that he was guilty of both murder and

treason. On December 2, 1859, Brown rode to the scaffold in Charles Town, Virginia, sitting on his own coffin in the back of a wagon. He was hanged in front of thousands of onlookers. However, that was not the end of the story. According to legend, the eyes of the dead Brown seemed to gleam as if he were still alive, causing the undertaker to seal them with wax after closing them.

More was to come. The house used as a hideout by Brown and his men before the raid was known as the Kennedy Farm, just south of Sharpsburg, Maryland. It is said that the sound of a group of men can be heard, either sleeping, talking, or moving up and down the farmhouse stairs.

Today Harpers Ferry is a popular tourist destination (now in West Virginia), and part of the old armory, including the engine house, is now owned by the National Park Service. Visitors to the town have mentioned encountering a reenactor bearing an uncanny resemblance to John Brown. The man seemed willing to pose for photographs in front of the engine house, and although taciturn, the tourists imagined that was simply him staying "in character." When the films were developed, the figure was nowhere to be seen.

When visitors mentioned the reenactor to local residents or Park Service employees, they were told that no such reenactor existed. Had these people encountered the restless ghost of John Brown? The same figure was also seen walking the street in front of the engine house at night, accompanied by a black dog like the one that accompanied Brown during the raid. Dog and man then

*Opposite: Harpers Ferry is reputedly home to several ghosts, not all of which are associated with John Brown's raid of 1859, though Brown himself is one of them.*

HARPER'S FERRY INSURRECTION—THE BATTLE GROUND—CAPTAIN ALBERTIS' PARTY ATTACKING THE INSURGENTS—VIEW OF THE RAILROAD BRIDGE, THE ENGINE-HOUSE AND THE VILLAGE.—FROM A SKETCH BY OUR SPECIAL ARTIST.

vanished through the door of the engine house. These stories would be more easily dismissed if they did not recur several times, and most residents are convinced that something otherworldly has become associated with Brown and his raid.

Another grisly ghost has also been associated with the raid. One of Brown's group was Dangerfield Newby, a free African American. During the first day of fighting, he was killed outside the gates of the armory, reputedly by an iron nail fired from a blunderbuss or shotgun. His body was left in the street, because it was too dangerous for anyone to approach the corpse due to the exchange of fire, so Newby's body was only recovered after the engine house was stormed. The corpse was simply tossed into an alleyway for the authorities to deal with, but according to the story,

pigs that inhabited the space between the buildings set upon the corpse and began eating its flesh. Ever since, the alley has been known as Hog Alley and has been home to a ghost that some identify with Dangerfield Newby. The figure of an African American man dressed in a slouch hat has been seen walking in the alleyway, his throat ripped open and bleeding. The figure then vanishes. Like so many ghost stories, there is little of substance to go on, but at least in this case the facts of Brown's raid are well known.

While many can dismiss these tales of the ghosts of Brown and one of his men as mere superstitious nonsense designed for the tourists and encouraged by nightly ghost tours, others remain convinced that there may be a fundamental bedrock of truth in the chilling tales.

*Above:* During the short siege of the engine house at Harpers Ferry, John Brown lost two of his sons in exchanges with local militia and townspeople, while Dangerfield Newby was killed somewhere outside the abolitionist's stronghold in the engine house.

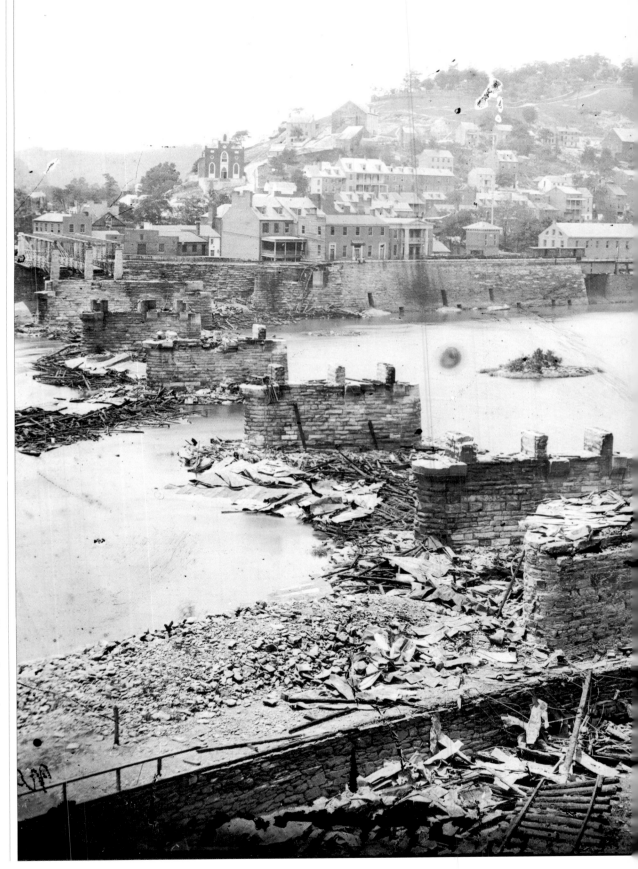

*Right: Harpers Ferry was occupied by both sides during the war and besieged by "Stonewall" Jackson during the Antietam campaign of September 1862. The Baltimore & Ohio Railroad bridge over the Potomac River was destroyed when the Confederates finally abandoned the town after the battle of Antietam.*

# GHOSTS OF THE EAST

LIKE SOME OF THE GHOST STORIES already mentioned, many of those of the eastern theater of war are unsubstantiated tales, where the only evidence for them ever occurring is local legend or the word of one or two individuals. Some may have a vested interest in stories of haunted houses, for example when people own the haunted property and run it as a guest house. Ghost stories are certainly good for business. However, there are many stories where there seems no ulterior motive, and the teller seems genuinely convinced that what they encountered was something in or from the realm of the supernatural. As important, places such as the Bloody Lane at Antietam, Devil's Den at Gettysburg, or the Sunken Lane at Fredericksburg are awe-inspiring locations, where the horrors that took place there during the Civil War are extremely easy to imagine. Even the most skeptical visitor can experience a sense of unease in these places, while others who are more willing to embrace the possibility of ghosts could find their imagination running away with them. What follows is a series of ghost stories from the great battlefields in Virginia, Maryland, and Pennsylvania, where the fate of America was decided. While some of these stories are easy to dismiss, others are a little more disturbing and are far harder to explain away.

*Left: The Devil's Den, Gettysburg, probably photographed by Alexander Gardner (some say Timothy O'Sullivan) and almost certainly "arranged." But the death was real enough.*

# The Ghosts of Antietam

*"He hid down at Snavely's Ford. I remember my grandpappy talking about it. What I'm saying is: It's just one generation."*

JERRY HOLSWORTH, ANTIETAM PARK RANGER, 1995

The small town of Sharpsburg in the northwestern corner of Maryland was the site of one of the bloodiest days of battle in the entire Civil War. On September 17, 1862, the Battle of Antietam was fought out in the rolling hills, small woods, and the lanes surrounding the town, a horrendous meat grinder of a battle that saw the Union Army of the Potomac launch successive assaults against Robert E. Lee's outnumbered and beleaguered Army of Northern Virginia. Given the appalling casualties inflicted on both sides during the battle, it is almost inevitable that Antietam has become associated with the ghosts of the combatants.

At Antietam, General McClellan's Union army enjoyed a distinct numerical advantage over the Confederates, the commander having some 80,000 men at his command to Lee's 50,000. Victory should have been assured. However, a string of poor tactical decisions meant that only part of this great army was launched into battle at any one time. Lee's line formed a crescent around Sharpsburg, with the Potomac River behind his army, preventing Lee's escape.

First McClellan launched Hooker's I Corps in an attack in the north across open cornfields toward the West Woods, but the Confederates held their ground. The fighting then switched to the center, where Sumner's II Corps and Porter's V Corps attacked Lee's weakly held line. The worst of the fighting took place along a sunken road, which soon earned the name "Bloody Lane." At one point, Union artillery was able to enfilade the Confederate position, turning the lane into an abattoir of blood and broken bodies before the guns could be driven off.

The slaughter in Bloody Lane was later regarded by veterans as probably the worst of the war. One of the several Union assaults is

**Below:** *After the battle, the Bloody Lane at Antietam was filled with the bodies of the combatants. Even today the site is a moving and distinctly eerie place.*

*Left: General George B. McClellan (1826–1885), or "Little Mac" as he was known led the Union Army of the Potomac from the summer of 1861 until he was removed from his command by President Lincoln following the Antietam campaign. During the battle he could have won the war in an afternoon, but instead he frittered away his huge numerical and tactical advantage by launching a series of piecemeal and costly frontal assaults on the Confederate position.*

particularly noteworthy, as the attackers included the veteran "Irish Brigade" from New York, part of Sumner's Corps. Led by their commander, General Meagher, the Irishmen were thrown into the fray just as an earlier Union attack began to falter. Cheering broke out from the Union ranks as the Irish Brigade advanced, its men calling out the brigade's war cry, "Faugh-a-Balaugh" ("Clear the Way" in Irish). With flags flying, the Irish Brigade advanced directly towards Bloody Lane, despite great gaps being ripped in its lines by Confederate fire. Meagher's horse was shot out from under him, but the general continued to attack on foot. The assault reached the lane, but by that time the Irishmen were all but broken, and after some fierce hand-to-hand fighting, the survivors were forced to fall back. The unit lost almost two-thirds of its force that day, some six hundred men. The Confederates were almost as badly mauled, and the dead lay four or five deep in the Bloody Lane.

Finally, Burnside's IX Corps attacked across Antietam Creek near a stone bridge, but a force of about four hundred Georgian sharpshooters managed to prevent the attackers from crossing the creek for almost four hours. Finally, after some heavy exchanges of fire and a gallant charge, a Union bridgehead was established on the far bank. By late afternoon it looked as if Lee's line would collapse under the pressure from Burnside, but in the nick of time, Confederate reinforcements arrived from Harpers Ferry, and the Union drive was stopped just short of Sharpsburg. The Confederates grimly held their ground until nightfall, despite mounting casualties on both sides, and Lee's battered army was able to escape back across the Potomac River the following day. The Confederate wounded were left behind in makeshift field hospitals at Sharpsburg's St. Paul's Lutheran Church or Grove Farm beyond the western outskirts of the town, but despite the best efforts of the surgeons, many died where they lay. A day of fighting that could have ended the Civil War then and there became just one more battle in a long conflict and an indecisive one that saw the highest number of casualties inflicted on America's young men in any one single day of fighting: over 22,000 soldiers were killed, wounded, or went missing during the battle.

Today the National Park Service owns large parts of the battlefield, and the site has been preserved so it looks pretty much the way it did during that fateful day in the early fall of 1862. Any visitor to the site with a modicum of imagination can gain an impression of what the battlefield must have looked like during the engagements, with the now empty fields filled with ragged lines of troops, fear-crazed horses, and thundering ordnance. Occasionally reenactment groups perform their drills and fight their mock battles on those formerly blood-soaked fields, making it even easier for visitors to step back in time.

For some, the experience is a little too real. Although tens of thousands of tourists visit the site every year, only a handful report experiencing anything other than the awe of standing in a spot where history was made. However, a few have experienced an even more moving visit to the battlefield. For

*Opposite: The lonley grave of John Marshall of Company L, the 28th Pennsylvania, near the West Woods at Antietam.*

*Right: Major General Winfield S. Hancock (seated) of the Union Army of the Potomac, pictured with three of his subordinate commanders in 1863. During the Battle of Antietam, Hancock led a brigade in Franklin's VI Corps.*

these few, the past really did seem to come alive for them.

Over the past century and a half, the sunken road known as Bloody Lane has come to represent the worst of the bloodletting on that September day in 1862, a potent symbol of both the ferocity of the fighting and the high cost of the battle in human lives. Even the most hardheaded of battlefield visitors would be hard-pressed not to acknowledge

*Left:* The Cornfield at Antietam was the scene of the first attacks of the day as Hooker and Mansfield launched their Union Corps across it into the Confederate lines located near this interpretive plaque. The field is still said to be haunted by the sounds of battle.

that Bloody Lane is an evocative and moving place, one where it is all to easy to imagine what happened there during the battle and which turned its whole length into a mass grave.

Even though I've visited hundreds of battlefields over the years, I have to acknowledge that this is an especially powerful spot. It is therefore little wonder that of all the places on the Antietam battlefield, Bloody Lane is the one where the majority of ghostly or supernatural phenomena have been encountered. The following are just a sample of these.

One of the most intriguing ghost stories associated with Bloody Lane centers around a school trip, when a group of Baltimore children visited the Antietam battlefield. The excursion from the McDonogh School in the northwestern Baltimore suburb of Owings Mills was one of several trips made to the battlefield by the school. One of the teachers, Frederick Maisel, was a former military interpreter for the Park Service, and his expertise

in military history helped bring the experience alive for the children. After giving them a demonstration on the common soldier of the period, Mr. Maisel and the trip leader Dennis O'Brien guided the students around the battlefield, an experience that culminated in a visit to Bloody Lane. The party marched down to the site just as dusk was falling, and this part of the trip was meant to be a reflective period, where the boys and girls were asked to reflect on what they had learned that day and on the events that had taken place on the ground on which they stood.

Mr. O'Brien told them to spread out in a line and not to talk during the thirty minutes of pondering in solitude. When they returned to the school, they would all be given a history assignment, for which they would be asked to record their feelings and experiences of the day. When the half hour was up, the students were called back, ready to board the school bus for the trip home.

It was then that several of the students approached the teachers and first told them

they had heard something strange, the sound of "chanting in a foreign-sounding voice." I contacted Mr. Maisel, who kindly added the following comment:

> When I asked them [the students] about this, it sounded to me like they said "Éire go brách!" That made the hairs on the back of my head stand up because I am quite familiar with the Irish Brigade who fought right there.

While the students almost certainly knew nothing of the Irish Brigade's war cry, as a military historian, Mr. Maisel was well aware of what the phrase meant and who used it. Because the children had been separated, there was also little chance of collusion between them, which is what makes the story all the more intriguing. The phrase, which is often anglicized to "Erin go Braugh," was a popular motto and war cry, literally meaning "Ireland the Good," although it is more usually translated as "Ireland Forever!" Most of the historic accounts refer to the Irish Brigade claim that the battle cry of the Irish soldiers that September day in 1862 was "Faugh-a-Balaugh," meaning "Clear the Way." However, to the non-Gaelic ear, the two chants would sound very similar, and in the heat of battle "Éire go brách" would be a far more inspiring war cry. Is it possible that the schoolchildren heard the sound of the ghosts of the Irish Brigade chanting "Ireland forever" or "Clear the Way"?

*Right: Although no ghost stories are directly associated with little Dunker Church in the middle of the battle-field, the fighting swirled around the Quaker meeting house and the West Woods beyond during the afternoon of the battle, and thousands of dead and wounded of both sides lay around it by the time the battle drew to a close.*

*Left: The Stone Bridge, or "Burnside's Bridge," on the southern side of the battlefield, is said to be haunted by mysterious ethereal lights and the ghostly sound of drumming. The bridge was the focal point of Burnside's attack throughout the morning of the battle, and Union casualties were heavy.*

Whatever the truth in the story, it seems indicative that Bloody Lane seems to attract strange and inexplicable events. If the event actually took place, did the students hear the ghosts of Meagher's men, or is there a less dramatic explanation for their account?

Their experience was certainly not the only unusual one associated with that blood-soaked spot. On a crisp warm day in September 1983, Lynn and Robert Scoville visited Antietam, as Robert was particularly interested in Civil War history. Having been raised in Virginia, Mrs. Scoville was used to Civil War battlefields and expected Antietam to be little different from all the others. They began their tour at the visitor center, touring the battlefield by car, following the driving trail set out by the National Park Service. It took them across the road to Dunker Church and then up past the Cornfield to the East Woods before looping back around to Bloody Lane. By that stage, Mrs. Scoville's interest had waned, and she remained in the car listening to the radio while her husband walked up to the interpretation panel behind Bloody Lane and switched on the audio commentary. Lynn Scoville recalled that "As we approached Bloody Lane, there were a lot of people milling about and taking pictures . . . I remember feeling a little bit annoyed because I was getting bored with it all and I wanted to hear the rest of the football game." The parking lot was immediately behind the southern end of the lane, and the car faced northeast across the fields beyond it, the ones the Union army crossed during its attack on the Confederate position. She got out of the car, enjoying the autumn sun and abandoning her football game she ambled toward her husband. Later, she described what followed:

I looked down at Bloody Lane, a rather unassuming sunken road, and then out at the fields beyond. What happened next is as clear in my mind as if it had happened yesterday. I don't know how to describe it except that it suddenly felt to me as if a filter had been put over the sun. The air temperature felt as though it dropped at least 20 degrees in a matter of seconds.

The sun was still shining brightly, the wind hadn't changed or increased, and yet I suddenly felt enveloped in a bone-chilling cold. At that same moment, I was overcome with such a powerful sense of death and abject terror my heart literally leaped into my throat. I dropped my eyes away from the battle site and stared directly at my feet, unable to look up. I knew, without a doubt in my mind, that if I were to look at the Bloody Lane at that moment I would see a sight so horrific that it would change my life forever.

*Right: Two drummer boys from the Union Army of the Potomac, photographed in 1862. The sound of ghostly drumming has been reported on several Civil War battlefields, including Shiloh, Bentonville, and Antietam. Do the ghosts of boys like these still haunt the sites of their last, terrifying ordeal?*

She then realized that although her husband and a dozen or so other people were in the same area, either in Bloody Lane, the parking lot, or the nearby observation platform, she seemed to be the only one who was experiencing the feeling. Looking anywhere but toward the lane and the fields beyond, she could see through her shielded eyes that everyone else was behaving completely normally. At that point, she recalls, "I broke out in a cold sweat and while still keeping my eyes averted, managed to grab Rob's arm and I shouted at him to take me back to the car. I was absolutely terrified and anxious to get away from there. Thinking I was sick, Rob took my arm and led me back to the car."

As the couple strode back to the car, Mrs. Scoville heard a loud, sharp metallic sound, a clanking that was repeated again and again, a bit, she later said, like someone striking a large cowbell. She was far too scared to turned around and see where the noise was coming from. She kept her eyes on the ground. Later she wondered if what she heard was the sound of bayonets clashing against each other, but without looking back she was never able find an explanation, supernatural or otherwise. Once safely in their car, Robert asked his wife what the matter was, but nearly hysterical, she just demanded that he drive. It was obvious his wife was extremely distressed, so they drove off and kept driving until they were clear of the National Park Service boundary. She recalled that:

It wasn't until we were outside the park that I told him what I had felt . . . He gave me a strange look but could tell by my shaken appearance it was not a good time to question my belief. I calmed down as we drove away and I was finally able to ask him if he had felt anything unusual. He said that he hadn't and that everything had seemed perfectly normal to him. I asked him incredulously about the metal clanging sound . . . surely he had heard that? He gave me another strange look and swore he had no idea what I was talking about.

It is widely believed that some people are more attuned to supernatural phenomena than others, or at least experience feelings that others are unable to share. While scientific experiments have neither proved nor disproved the validity of this, popular belief and tradition seems to support the notion. One doesn't have to believe in the "sixth sense" or have experienced inexplicable feelings such as those Mrs. Scoville had that day to consider it possible that in the same way as some people are more intuitive than others or can read people's moods better than the rest of us, some people are more susceptible to such feelings than most of the people around them. While it is all too easy to dismiss such notions, Mrs. Scoville was completely unaware that she might have had any particular supernatural powers until she drove into the parking lot at Bloody Lane.

Apart from Bloody Lane, there are three other locations on or near the battlefield associated with ghosts. The stone bridge over Antietam Creek, which was later dubbed "Burnside's Bridge," has had its share of strange occurrences. After the battle, it has been suggested that some of the Union troops who fell during the repeated attempts to cross the creek were left behind by the burial parties, as their bodies were hidden in woods or thickets or had been carried downstream to be lodged along the banks of the creek. While these dead soldiers were found in the days that followed, it is claimed that many of them were simply buried in unmarked graves close to where the bodies were discovered. Some suggest that their restless souls still haunt the same woods and thickets, searching for their comrades who lie in the official cemetery. It has also been claimed that on some nights, faint blue lights can be seen moving through the trees along the creek before the lights disappear into the darkness. Even more intriguingly, it has also been claimed that sometimes a drum can be heard beating out a slow cadence, and after a short while the beat slowly fades away. Without having spent the night next to Burnside's Bridge and experiencing these reported phenomena, it would be

hard to dismiss these stories. However, a handful of people, including park rangers, are convinced that what they heard or saw was genuine.

Four buildings have supernatural associations with the battle. One of these is the Phillip Pry House, a brick farmhouse on the northeastern side of the battlefield that served as the headquarters of the Union commander General McClellan during the Battle of Antietam. A surgical unit was attached to the Army of the Potomac's headquarters, and senior officers who were wounded were often taken there rather than to the main casualty centers, where the generals would have had to lie alongside the men under their command. General Hooker's I Corps attacked soon after dawn, and the

*Above:* St. Paul's Lutheran Church in Sharpsburg is still said to be haunted by the ghosts of wounded Confederate soldiers, and strange lights can sometimes be seen from the building's bell tower. The church served as a field hospital during the battle, and this photograph was taken shortly afterwards.

*Above: Grove Farm is best remembered as the site of the meeting between President Lincoln and General McClellan after the battle, but during the fighting it was used as a casualty clearing station. The blood of wounded Confederate soldiers is still said to stain the floorboards of the farmhouse, and no amount of scrubbing can ever remove it.*

intensity of the fighting in or near the Cornfield that followed stunned everyone who lived to tell the tale. As Hooker himself recalled: "Every stalk of corn in the northern and greater part of the field was cut as closely as could have been done with a knife, and the slain lay in rows as precisely as they had stood in their ranks a moment before." Shortly afterward, the general was hit in the foot and taken to McClellan's headquarters to be treated. The cull of the senior Union officers continued until the afternoon, when a divisional commander of II Corps, General Israel Richardson, was felled from his horse near Bloody Lane.

Severely wounded in the stomach, he was taken to the Phillip Pry House to be treated by McClellan's surgeons, who declared there

was little they could do for him. The general would remain in the house for another six months before he succumbed to his wounds on November 3, 1862.

The house is now owned by the National Park Service, although it is closed to visitors. It was used for storage until 1976, when the building caught fire, the blaze destroying a portion of the structure. The National Park Service decided to restore the building, which was when the first strange occurrence took place. During a planning meeting by park staff held in an upstairs room, the wife of one of the participants entered the house and began ascending the stairs to join her husband. She then noticed a woman coming down, so she stepped back out of the way to let her pass. The woman was clearly a reenactor, as she was dressed in a long period dress. When the wife spoke to her husband later, she mentioned the reenactor lady and was surprised to learn that no such reenactor had been at the meeting. Had she met a ghost on the stairs?

A few weeks later, when contractors moved in to start the rebuilding of the damaged wing of the farmhouse, they reported seeing a woman looking out of an upstairs window as they first approached the farmhouse. When they arrived, they discovered that the room where the lady was standing was part of the house that had been damaged in the fire, and the upstairs room where she had been standing had no floor! Unless the woman had been clinging to the inside shell of the farmhouse, then, they concluded, they had seen a ghost, who bore a striking similarity to the figure seen on the stairs. The upstairs room was also

the one where General Richardson had been taken after the battle and where he later died. The mystery woman was immediately associated with Frances ("Fannie") Richardson, the wife of the general who cared for him during the six months he lay dying. After another encounter, the contractors abandoned the job, and the work was finished by a new and perhaps less sensitive group of builders.

Other ghostly activity in the house also involves the staircase, where footsteps have been heard climbing, descending, or pacing in the lobby at their foot. Some have claimed the ghostly footsteps are those of Mrs. Richardson, while others are convinced they belong to men, perhaps McClellan's staff moving around the building immediately before the battle that cost the lives of so many.

Finally, there are the three buildings used as makeshift hospitals for Robert E. Lee's Army of Northern Virginia: St. Paul's Lutheran Church, Grove Farm, and the Piper House. The church stands near the center of the small town of Sharpsburg, immediately behind the Confederate right, and during September 17, 1862, a steady stream of casualties flowed through its doors. The building was badly damaged by Union artillery during the engagement, and conditions in the church must have been appalling, with the dead and dying lying everywhere as surgeons tried to work while shells struck the building above them, and the piles of amputated limbs grew steadily throughout the day. The church was repaired and later rebuilt in the years that followed, but according to Sharpsburg residents, the groans and cries of the wounded and dying soldiers could still occasionally be heard coming from the interior of the church. Others report seeing some strange blue lights flickering from the tower of the church, a description reminiscent of the lights seen near Burnside's Bridge.

Grove Farm lies a half mile to the west of Sharpsburg, and it too was used as a Confederate casualty station. Later, McClellan set up a temporary headquarters beside the farm, and the farmhouse served as the backdrop in a posed photograph when President Lincoln visited McClellan's headquarters there on October 3, 1862.

The story goes that the floorboards of the farmhouse are still stained with the blood of the wounded, and that no amount of vigorous scrubbing has ever managed to remove the marks.

The last of the three buildings is the Piper House, located a quarter of a mile southwest of Bloody Lane, midway between the lane and the northern outskirts of Sharpsburg. The farmhouse served as the headquarters of General Longstreet during the battle, and it also served as a temporary casualty station.

The fighting came so close to this Confederate headquarters that three soldiers were killed when sheltering inside the building during the battle.

Although the current owners of the property no longer open their house to the public, for several years they ran the farm as a guest house, providing an attractive setting for those interested in Civil War history.

Although Mr. and Mrs. Clark, who own the house, remain skeptics, they do admit that several of their guests have encountered rather more of the Civil War than they would have expected or perhaps liked.

Inexplicably, these ghostly encounters all took place in a part of the farmhouse that was built forty years after the battle was fought. Guests have reported hearing voices from there and strange sounds, and some claim to have seen a ghostly apparition who appeared in a doorway.

The owners can offer no explanation and themselves remain unconvinced by these reports and stories, although one theory is that the extension to the house was built over the unmarked graves of unknown Confederate soldiers, and the ghosts are those of the dead seeking peace.

Much of this might be explained by the fact that many of the guests are unused to sleeping in old historic houses, and thus their experiences might have had more to do with bad dreams brought on by their surroundings than anything else.

Mr. Clark himself claims to have slept in every room in the house and never experienced any such goings on.

Like so many stories of this kind, they are almost impossible to prove, and those who want to believe in ghosts will do so. One thing is certain though, which is that Antietam is a particularly moving Civil War battlefield, partly because of its near pristine condition, which makes it that much more evocative, and partly through awareness of the bloody dramas that unfolded there.

It is little wonder that some people experience something spiritual in such a hallowed and tragic place.

# Ghosts of Fredericksburg

*"A chicken could not live on that field when we open on it."*
PORTER ALEXANDER, COMMANDER OF THE ARTILLERY BATTALION AT FREDERICKSBURG

After the lost opportunity of Antietam, President Lincoln removed General McClellan from command of the Army of the Potomac and replaced him with Major-General Ambrose E. Burnside, who until then had commanded IX Corps. Burnside was a surprising choice, as he had done little to distinguish himself in the war so far. However, he had proved himself to be loyal to his superiors, dedicated to the war effort, and free from political associations. As Lee withdrew his army south through Virginia to the relative safety of the south bank of the Rappahannock River, McClellan and then

Burnside had slowly followed behind, seemingly unwilling to bring their army into action. By mid-November, Burnside's Army of the Potomac was gathered on the north bank of the Rappahannock opposite the town of Fredericksburg, while Lee's troops held the high ground on the far side of the river. Any further Union advance was delayed until pontoon bridges could be brought up to allow the army to cross the river, so it was December before Burnside was able to make his move. On the night of December 10, the Union army sent a detachment across the river that drove the Confederate soldiers back

*Left: Fredericksburg, viewed from the ruins of the railroad bridge across the Rappahannock River when the Confederates rebuilt the structure in the summer of 1863. The town is thought to be one of the most haunted in America.*

*Right: Union skirmishers cross the river to drive back Confederate sharpshooters during the opening stages of the Battle of Fredericksburg in December 1862. The ghost of a young Union soldier who haunts the Willis House is supposed to be that of one of these Union skirmishers.*

from it. For the next few days, Union engineers spanned the river in two places, with three pontoon bridges spanning the Rappahannock at Fredericksburg, and three more about two thousand yards downstream. At dawn on December 13, Burnside ordered his army into battle, with Sumner's "grand division" of two corps crossing into Fredericksburg while Franklin's two corps crossed further downstream. The advance began as soon as the troops deployed on the southern bank of the river.

First, Couch's II Corps attacked west across the open rising ground between Fredericksburg and the Confederate lines at Marye's Heights, while Reynolds probed to the southwest from Franklin's position south of the town. The attack on Marye's Heights proved a costly failure, as the attackers were cut down or stopped before they could get near the Confederate front line, a sunken road running along the base of the hill. Throughout the rest of the day, while Franklin and Reynolds traded shots with the Confederate defenders of Prospect Hill to the south, Sumner and then Hooker (commanding III Corps and IX Corps) launched repeated frontal attacks against the Confederate position. In fact, fourteen separate attacks were made, and all met the same fate. All these Union assaults were easily repulsed by the Confederates, and unit after unit was either cut down or broke and ran. Often running wasn't an option, as to do so would have invited certain death at the hands of the Confederate muskets. Instead, thousands of troops hugged the open ground and prayed for nightfall. Dusk brought an end to the fighting, but the suffering continued as thousands of wounded or dying troops lay between the two armies, while those who could move limped back across the river to safety. The Battle of Fredericksburg proved to be a clear and overwhelming Confederate victory, but it was bought at a terrible price.

The Confederates lost some 5,580 men during the battle, the majority from long-range Union artillery fire or in the close-quarters fighting on the lower slopes of Prospect Hill between "Stonewall" Jackson's corps and the Union troops south of the town. As for the Army of the Potomac, it suffered 12,600 casualties that day. Of these, some 6,300 men were killed, seriously wounded, or went missing during the assaults on Marye's Heights. It was a death toll that almost rivaled that at Antietam three months before. It also ensured that Robert E. Lee's army would survive through the winter, and its morale was buoyed by victory.

Like so many Civil War battlefields, it is extremely easy to stand in certain spots and imagine what went on there during the battle. Even though modern houses cover the ground to the east of the sunken road, the National Park Service has preserved enough of the Confederate position to allow visitors to gain an impression of what the scene would have been like. For some people, the past has very much come alive.

The Willis House in Fredericksburg was built in the 1740s by John Allan, a Scottish-born merchant, and it remains one of the few houses to survive both the American Revolution and the Civil War. The property on Princess Anne Street was added to over the years, its present name was derived from its postwar owners, and members of the Willis family have lived in the house since the turn of the nineteenth century.

On December 11, General Burnside ordered the Union guns across the river on Stafford Heights to bombard the town, in an attempt to drive out the Confederate sharpshooters who were harassing the army's bridg-

*Left: Major General Thomas J. "Stonewall" Jackson (1824–1863) played a prominent role in the battle, masterminding the defense of the southern part of the Confederate line near Mansfield House. The ghosts of the men under his command are still said to haunt the battlefield.*

ing engineers. The town soon lay in ruins, and hundreds of residents fled for their lives towards the main Confederate lines to the west. Surprisingly, the Willis House emerged largely unscathed, and when the Union army crossed the river in force on December 13, it remained one of the few buildings that had not been reduced to a charred ruin.

According to the Willis family, a young Union soldier entered the house that morning, but while he was hiding from enemy fire behind one the double doors in the back hall, a bullet ripped a splinter through the door at chest height and killed him. The hole was later plugged, but traces of the damage can still be seen today. The soldier was later buried in the garden. During the 1920s, Mrs. Marian Willis was living in the house together with her cook Nannie. The family claim that on several occasions Nannie saw the young soldier enter the house from the porch through a side door, then either disap-

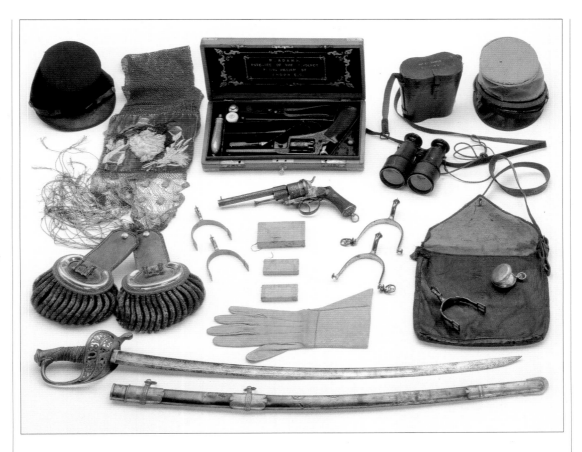

*Right:* The personal effects of General Stonewall Jackson include two of his forage caps, his plain Model 1850 sword, and his dress epaulettes from the Virginia Military Institute. His ghost is still said to haunt the grounds of the military college in Lexington.

pear or move up the stairs. When she first saw him, she thought it was her employer's younger brother, but when she looked closer, she saw the youngster wore a Union uniform. The two women eventually nicknamed him "Yip the Yank."

Eventually, Nannie decided to take matters into her own hands and try to "lay his soul to rest." She went to the site of the grave in the garden and prayed, then tried to persuade his soul to rest in peace and that a corner of a garden in Fredericksburg was a perfectly suitable resting place for him, even though the grave remained unmarked and the soldier unidentified. The ghost was never seen again.

Others have reported strange happenings in the town that boasts that it is the "Most Historic City in America." Many residents claim to have heard the sound of men's alarmed voices, although nobody could be seen. Others report hearing bullets whiz past

them in the street. As one resident put it: "One thing that you may have several people verify is the bullets. There is a phenomenon where bullets come up through the street[s]. I haven't found one yet but I was with my neighbor as they found one." A few have even seen groups of men marching in Civil War uniforms or advancing in skirmish lines through the streets. It was thought that these soldiers were reenactors, until they vanished into thin air. Residents in the area at the foot of Marye's Heights where the main Union attacks were made have also reported seeing things. As one resident recalled:

I now live one house from the corner of William Street and Sunken Road. As you might know this was the site of a horrific battle where hundreds of Union soldiers were killed trying to rush the natural cover of the "Sunken Road." The area is also called Maryes Heights. On one occasion I have seen what I believed to

be a soldier stumbling (maybe wounded) back down the hill. It was one of those times where you see it and keep going, then you look back and it's gone. I seem to recall seeing a young man in the clothes of the soldier in what I would call a haze. Another time I was riding a scooter down Sunken Road toward Lafayette Blvd. [through the Battlefield Park and alongside the cemetery]. As I was passing the stand of trees with the Sunken Road wall on my right, I thought I heard men speaking in a panic, like they were amidst the chaos of battle.

The same man also recounted another bizarre story, this time involving an inanimate object rather than a ghost.

On another occasion I was window-shopping downtown with my fiancée one afternoon. As we walked the sidewalk we saw several small tables on which were placed some items for sale. At quick glance there was nothing of interest so we went on. As we walked past we heard a bell ringing. We stopped, backtracked and looked to see what it was. On one of the tables there was a bell suspended from a wooden stand on a small wire with some engraving on it. As we looked, it continued to ring. We inspected it closely to see where the batteries, string, wire, or antenna (for remote control) was. Upon close inspection we could not find any means of outside intervention at all! We also peered into the store to see if anyone was watching us to see our reaction. There was no one watching at all. No "Candid Camera."

It is all too easy to dismiss the testimony of one man when it comes to supernatural experiences, but the problem with Fredericksburg is that numerous residents have had similar experiences. The difficulty comes in determining who is genuine in retelling what they saw or heard, and who is simply a crank. For example, the following account can be interpreted either way.

In 1749, Mann Page, a member of Virginia's House of Burgesses, built a mansion called Mansfield a mile and a half south of the town. During the battle, it lay within the enclave occupied by Franklin's "grand division," and although the property survived the battle without suffering much

*Below: The sunken lane at Marye's Heights, photographed after the successful storming of the position by overwhelming numbers of Union troops in May 1863, when Lee's main army was fighting and winning the Battle of Chancellorsville a few miles to the west.*

damage, it was badly damaged by fire a year later. Today the building is in private hands, sitting within its own wooded grounds just off Tidewater Trail, next to the Fredericksburg Country Club. During the battle, the building served as both a headquarters and a casualty station, and it was later reoccupied by Confederate troops, who maintained an outpost there throughout the spring of 1863.

Over the years, several locals claim to have seen the ghostly apparition of a group of Confederate soldiers in the grounds of the house, although according to the local ghost tour staff, the bulk of these reports were made by one particular lady during the 1980s, a neighbor who declared that she had psychic and clairvoyant powers. She claims that she repeatedly saw a group of Confederate riders, dismounted and either standing guard around the house itself or tending to their horses tethered in the trees.

The accuracy of her claims cannot be verified, since it proved impossible to trace the lady. Was she just a cranky old lady, or did she really see something few others could share? Just as Fredericksburg might lay claim to being the most historic city in America, it also seems to be the one that can boast the greatest frequency of ghostly happenings associated with the Civil War.

# Ghosts of Gettysburg

*"On great fields something stays. Forms change and pass;*
*bodies disappear, but spirits linger, to consecrate ground for*
*the vision-place of souls."*
    COLONEL J. L. CHAMBERLAIN, MONUMENT DEDICATION, GETTYSBURG, OCTOBER 3, 1889

The three days of Gettysburg (July 1–3, 1863) were probably the most decisive of the entire Civil War. The battle fought on these rolling Pennsylvania fields decided the fate of the two combatants, and marked the high point of the Southern cause. Until then, the tide of victory lay with the Confederacy, but after the carnage of Gettysburg, Lee's battered and outnumbered Army of Northern Virginia was on the defensive and would be pushed ever further south until the war reached its weary conclusion in April 1865. The army's belief in its commander and its own abilities were replaced by a realization that despite their best efforts, they were unable to stop the overwhelming numbers of the Union army.

The battle came about as a result of Lee's second invasion of the North. The first invasion the year before almost ended in disaster at Antietam, and only the ineptitude of the Union command allowed Lee's army to escape back into Virginia. This time Lee led his army across the Potomac River and marched northward into Pennsylvania, in an attempt to bring about a decisive battle on ground of his own choosing and well away from the war-ravaged soil of Virginia. Unknowingly, the two great armies converged on the small crossroads town of Gettysburg: Lee's 77,000 men spread over miles of enemy countryside, while Meade's 94,000-strong Army of the Potomac raced westward to intercept the Confederate army. Early in the morning of July 1, the Confederate vanguard clashed with a screen of dismounted Union cavalry to the west of the town, and on both sides, reinforcements marched to the sound of the guns until the skirmish had developed into a full-scale battle. As night fell, the Confederates succeeded in breaking the Union line and drove the shattered defenders back through Gettysburg into the hills beyond. Fresh Union troops had already established a line running along this line of low hills and ridges: a fishhook-shaped front running from Culp's Hill to Cemetery Hill immediately south of Gettysburg itself, then running southeast along Cemetery Ridge towards two rocky outcrops known as Round Top and Little Round Top. General Ewell called off the Confederate pursuit, and as reinforcements arrived throughout the night, both Lee and Meade planned for a renewal of the battle the following day.

By dawn on July 2, it was clear that the Union army would remain on the defensive, holding its deceptively strong position on Cemetery Ridge. Lee decided to launch a pinning attack against Culp's Hill, the barb of the fishhook, with Ewell's corps, while General Longstreet would launch his own corps against the southern end of the Union line, towards Little Round Top. Although Ewell achieved little, and although the southern attack only began in late afternoon, Longstreet managed to drive the Union defenders out of key defensive areas known as the "Peach Orchard" and the "Wheatfield." By early evening, his men were standing in Plum Run, a creek at the foot of Little Round Top. Longstreet then launched repeated attacks up the hill, and the fighting

*Opposite: The Wheatfield changed hands several times during the furious fighting of the battle's second day, and the spot is still supposed to be haunted by the ghost of General Barksdale, a Confederate brigade commander from Mississippi.*

*Right:* The Army of the Potomac's chief engineer Brigadier General G.K. Warren pictured on top of Little Round Top during the battle. He realized the importance of the feature, and both sides funneled men into the hand-to-hand battle for the hill. Its summit is now said to be haunted by their ghosts.

on Little Round Top and nearby Devil's Den was bitter: hand-to-hand engagements using muskets, bayonets, and bare hands. The Confederates were driven back shortly before nightfall, and Lee ordered Longstreet to pull back to try again the following day.

More reinforcements continued to arrive, and by July 3, it was clear that the Union line was all but impregnable. Most commanders would have broken off the battle there and then, but Lee and his men still believed they could outfight the enemy, and still had an

unswerving belief in their own abilities. Consequently, at three in the afternoon, Lee launched one final attack, a massed assault against the relatively weakly held center of the Union line on Cemetery Ridge. This assault of over 13,000 Confederates would go down in history as Pickett's Charge, named after the commander of the leading division. The attackers had to cross a mile of open ground, and for much of the time they were within range of the enemy guns. Despite appalling casualties, a few of Pickett's men reached the Union line, but they were soon repulsed by Union reserves. As the survivors staggered back to the Confederate lines, it was clear that the battle was lost. Lee withdrew his battered army under cover of darkness and led his men back into Virginia. The Confederate dream ended that day, and some of Lee's best veteran troops lay where they had fallen on the blood-soaked open ground in front of Cemetery Ridge or amid the trees and rocks of Little Round Top and Devil's Den. Over 50,000 lives were claimed or ruined by serious wounds during the battle or during its aftermath: 28,000 Confederate and 22,000 Union casualties making it the bloodiest battle of the war.

Nearly a century and a half later, the town of Gettysburg still lies in the shadow of that great climactic battle. Tourists come in the thousands to see where it all happened, and the National Park Service has preserved a large portion of the Union line, albeit an area scarred by dozens of monuments erected by both the victors and the vanquished. The town also provides guidance for those who

are interested in other aspects of the battle's aftermath; two ghost tours give tourists the opportunity to visit the sites where the battle raged and where it is claimed that some of the combatants are still reliving their last moments. Gettysburg is an awe-inspiring place. I saw one visitor from North Carolina openly weep at the spot marking the "High Water Mark of the Confederacy," where Pickett's men reached the Union line at a spot known as "Bloody Angle." The view from Little Round Top or Devil's Den is much the same as it was in 1863, making it easy to imagine what happened on those rocky, tree-covered slopes. For many visitors, history comes alive at Gettysburg.

Less readily apparent, the battlefield and its environs are also considered to be one of the most haunted places in America, and given the momentous events that took place there, it is easy to see why it could gain such a reputation.

During the first day of the battle, the fighting moved through Gettysburg itself, and afterward the town became a huge hospital, filled with the dying and the wounded of both sides. It is inevitable that the town itself has its fair share of ghost stories. One of these involves the Farnsworth House on Baltimore Street, a modest structure built in 1810 by local merchant John McFarland and modified over the intervening two centuries. For the past century, the building has been used as a restaurant and guest house—the Farnsworth House Inn. After the Confederates occupied the town, the building was taken over by Confederate sharpshooters, and

*Above: The "High Water Mark of the Confederacy," Bloody Angle, on top of Cemetery Ridge. This was the target for Pickett's Charge, and after the engagement, the wall in front of the guns and the fields leading to it were covered in Confederate dead.*

during the next two days these men fired on Union positions on Cemetery Hill from the house's attic. A stray shot from one of these marksmen also killed Jennie Wade in the nearby Sweeney House, the only known civilian casualty of the battle. According to local legend, the sharpshooters can still be heard in the attic, and the sound of a Jew's harp can be heard as the soldiers still while away the hours in the top of the house. After the battle, the southern side of the house facing Cemetery Hill was marked by over a hundred bullet holes, showing that the Union troops returned the fire of the Confederate sharpshooters. Other inexplicable sounds or apparitions have also been seen in the house

over the years—ghostly figures or shadows appearing in bedrooms or public rooms, footsteps on the empty stairs, and the impression of movement out of the corner of an eye—but when the person turns, there is nothing to be seen. Members of staff have even been touched by an unseen hand or brushed into by passing and invisible figures. These kinds of tales are fairly typical of the nonspecific haunting tales associated with many old houses, fabricated or otherwise.

What makes the tales from the Farnsworth House particularly intriguing is that guests with no interest in such matters have reported encounters of this kind, while the staff is adamant that something strange is

*Left: Today, these gently rolling Pennsylvania fields appear tranquil, but over 150 years ago they echoed with the sound of battle. Do some of those long-lost soldiers still linger on these fields today?*

associated with the house. For instance, waitresses in the inn's restaurant have had their aprons tugged by unseen hands, and on one occasion, the effects were witnessed by many of the diners in the restaurant. Another member of the waitstaff saw a tray of silverware move as if being picked up by an invisible person before it was thrown to the floor.

Staff members have seen the figure of a woman in mid-nineteenth-century costume who appeared to be looking for something in a downstairs hallway, who then vanished. The same figure has been seen by others, both guests and staff, many of whom were unaware of the stories surrounding the property. There may indeed be something to these tales, but they have become so entrenched in the popular history of the house that it is difficult to separate fact from fiction.

Farnsworth House nevertheless remains one of the most haunted buildings associated with any Civil War battlefield, and it also features as an important stop on Gettysburg's ghost tours.

Another supposedly haunted building is Pennsylvania Hall, an impressive red-roofed building with a white colonnaded frontage standing in the middle of the campus of Gettysburg College, on the northern outskirts of the town. In 1863, the college (then known as Pennsylvania College) consisted of just the hall and two other buildings, and these were used as field hospitals by the Confederates during the battle, while an observation point was probably established in the building's central cupola. The hall itself now houses the administrative offices of the college, but during those three days in July 1863, things must have looked very different, as bodies lay in rows outside the building and wounded were being brought in to the blood-soaked hall for treatment. Many never survived the ordeal, and the scene inside its walls must have been horrendous. According to the stories, both staff and students have seen the outlines of people watching them from the hall cupola. Upon investigation, it turned out that nobody was up there.

Some reported seeing what looked like Confederate soldiers in the cupola, so the top of the building developed a reputation for being haunted by the ghosts of Lee's soldiers. An even more alarming story concerns two members of the campus administration who rode the elevator down from the top floor of Pennsylvania Hall one evening after work. Inexplicably, the elevator passed the lobby level of the building and continued on to the basement. When the doors opened, they found they'd arrived in the basement, only it was the basement as it would have looked during the battle. Bodies and wounded Confederate soldiers lay everywhere, while blood-splattered surgeons and medical orderlies worked to save those they could.

The men in the elevator desperately punched the buttons, and the doors closed, but not before an orderly looked up from his work and looked at them imploringly, as if asking for their help. The two staff members later recalled that there was no sound in the basement, as if what they witnessed was a movie with the sound turned down. This was a shared experience by two reliable witnesses who never believed in such things until that evening. According to the local Gettysburg author and ghost tour–guide Mark Nesbitt, the two men continued to work in the campus building, but from then on they took the stairs. The two men who witnessed the scene have declined to share their experiences with only a few people, including Nesbitt, so the

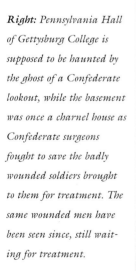

*Right: Pennsylvania Hall of Gettysburg College is supposed to be haunted by the ghost of a Confederate lookout, while the basement was once a charnel house as Confederate surgeons fought to save the badly wounded soldiers brought to them for treatment. The same wounded men have been seen since, still waiting for treatment.*

accuracy of their testimony is difficult to verify. Their reticence is in a kind of a way more convincing than open testimony: it implies that they know what they saw but won't be interrogated about it, since they would probably not be believed and look like they're crazy. There remains the possibility that what they saw was some sort of manifestation of the most traumatic episode in the building's history.

While these two buildings may claim to be haunted by ghosts of the Civil War, their claims pale into insignificance compared to the tales associated with the Cashtown Inn, some eight miles northwest of the battlefield, just off the Gettysburg to Chambersburg Road. General Heth, who commanded the Confederate vanguard, established his headquarters there on July 1, and the bulk of the army's senior officers gathered at the inn that evening. It was here that Lee and his staff met after the first day of the battle, and the Confederate commander made the momentous decision to attack the Union position the following day.

The ghost stories linked to the Cashtown Inn are legion. One concerns a local doctor who was passing the inn one night shortly before World War 1 when he was accosted by a man dressed like a Confederate soldier. The man forced the doctor to accompany him into some nearby woods, where he came across a wounded man, bleeding from a gunshot wound. The doctor was released after he treated the man. The following day, all traces of the wounded man and his companion had gone. Had he treated a ghost or just a

wounded transient or robber? The story goes that the same thing happened to another doctor several years later, and once again there was no trace of the soldiers and their temporary bivouac the following morning.

Guests at the inn have reported several strange experiences: mysterious footsteps in the attic, freezingly cold spots in an otherwise warm room, inexplicable images appearing in photographs, doors opening or closing without reason, or the sound of furniture being moved around their rooms. Previous owners of the inn recalled how one guest was kept awake by knocking at his door. Whenever he got out of bed to investigate, there was no one there. Another heard the sound of horses outside the window, but once again there was nothing to be seen. Several guests over the years have mentioned seeing a figure dressed as a Confederate soldier in the hall, in a certain bedroom, or behind the bar. It has been suggested that this figure is the ghost of a Confederate soldier who was killed by a Union sniper as the Confederate vanguard passed through the hills just to the west of Cashtown, and he was brought to the inn to die.

*Above: The death of Major General John Reynolds, the commander of Union I Corps, near the Chambersburg Pike during the first day of the battle. Ghosts are still said to haunt the spot, the first sighted by a seventy-five-year-old veteran, John Burns, who reported encountering the ghost of a Confederate soldier there just a few years after the end of the war.*

*Above: Gettysburg, viewed from the Chambersburg Pike where it crosses Seminary Ridge just to the west of the town. From there, the road leads into the Cashtown Road, down which the lead units of Lee's army advanced on July 1, 1863. Close by is the site of the haunted Thompson Barn.*

If the inn isn't haunted in some way, then it seems difficult to explain why so many different guests and visitors have experienced these strange occurrences. While much of this might have to do with expectation, and many people stay there in the hope of encountering something unusual, the sheer volume of accounts suggests something more mysterious might be behind at least some of these events.

A half mile to the west, the Thompson Farm on Seminary Ridge lies beside the Chambersburg Pike, and although the neighboring McPherson Farm bore the brunt of the first day of fighting on July 1, the home of the widowed Mary Thompson also suffered damage during the fighting that day. The Union cavalry line that first halted the Confederate vanguard was deployed a little to the west, and during the later stages of the battle, first the retreating Union troops and then the advancing Confederates of General Ambrose P. Hill's corps passed through the farmyard. During the next few days, the farm served as General Lee's headquarters, and both parts of the house and the barn adjacent to it were turned into casualty stations.

During the battle, the dead must have stacked up like cordwood in the back of the farmyard. Four days later, after the battle-weary Confederate army had marched away, Union burial parties moved in to intern the dead. One such pile of bodies lay in a shallow pit beside the Thompson Barn, and one by one, the bodies were removed. When the burial party reached the bottom of the stack, they grabbed one of the few remaining corpses, only to see his limbs move of their own accord and his eyes snap open. The soldier was still alive, having spent four days underneath a pile of corpses rotting and becoming bloated in the sun. The poor figure began to scream, which was more than enough for the Union troops, who fled the scene. Eventually, they returned with a doctor, who examined the man and declared he had been driven insane by his experience. The injured and demented soldier died of his wounds and his near-death experience two days later and was buried with the rest of his comrades.

The barn was destroyed in a fire a few decades later, and a new building was constructed on the site. This new farm building boasted an earthen storage cellar, and the

occupants regularly heard strange noises coming from it—mostly the sound of groaning but also the creaking of what sounded like wagon wheels. Matters came to a head when everyone in the house was woken by a sound not unlike a roaring furnace coming from the cellar. The whole house began shaking. When they entered the cellar, they found the noise was coming from the far end, where an oak door separated one part of the basement from the other. It seemed as if someone was battering the door from the far side, and as they watched, the door crashed off its hinges, revealing an empty room beyond. This was enough for the occupants, who fled the house. They called in a clergyman who specialized in hauntings and strange occurrences, and he inspected the house then blessed it. He later told the family that the spirit was one who should be pitied, a Confederate soldier who had been buried alive on the spot, but whose soul was now at rest. No further incidents were ever reported, and the once-haunted property now forms part of the Lutheran Seminary's estate. I've tried without success to find any hard evidence that a

Confederate soldier was ever buried alive near the Thompson Barn, and despite searching several relevant sets of medical records, no account of a doctor treating such a man has been found. However, several medical references mention soldiers driven mad during the battle and even describe the symptoms, a relatively new phenomenon—or at least a new observation—in the mid-nineteenth century. Whatever lies behind this story, the Thompson Farm certainly played host to some macabre events during those few days in the summer of 1863.

In addition to the places where casualty stations were established behind the opposing lines, certain areas of the battlefield itself have their own fair share of ghostly associations. Allegedly, Devil's Den is far and away the most haunted spot on the Gettysburg battlefield. According to local lore, the area was once the site of an earlier battle, fought between two rival Native American tribes, an engagement known as the "Battle of the Crows." A nineteenth-century local historian, Emmanuel Bushman, claimed that many supernatural sights and sounds had been

*Left: Monuments to the fallen, such as this one dedicated to the North Carolinians, punctuate the battlefield of Gettysburg. It seems as if almost as many ghosts still remain on the battlefields as there are monuments. Gettysburg is widely regarded as one of the most haunted battlefields of the war.*

experienced there long before the Civil War battle, and secret Native American ceremonies were held on the site. He also stated that the area was alternatively known as the "Indian Fields," an old association with the earlier battle, although he failed to track down how Devil's Den got its name.

On July 2, 1863, Devil's Den marked the southern end of the Union line, a position held by Ward's Brigade of General Sickles's III Corps. When the Confederates attacked, the assault quickly degenerated into a series of skirmishes fought at close quarters within the jumble of boulders, while artillerymen and sharpshooters on Little Round Top added their fire in support of the troops down below. At one stage, the defenders were forced back to the very summit of Little Round Top before a countercharge spear-

headed by Colonel Chamberlain's Maine Regiment turned the tide of battle. A second Confederate attack was stopped among the boulders, and despite a Union counterattack, Devil's Den remained in Confederate hands until Longstreet gave the order to pull back as darkness brought an end to the fighting.

By that time the boulders of Devil's Den had become death markers, with bodies of both sides wedged between the rocks. That night Union troops tried to recover what bodies they could find and tend to the wounded, but given the darkness and the jumbled landscape, the task proved impossible. A few days after the battle, the burial parties arrived at Devil's Den, and it took them several days to locate and bury the dead. It was later claimed that some of the Confederate dead weren't buried at all, just

*Below: This selection of photographic portraits of Confederate commanders includes that of William Barksdale (1821–1863), whose ghost is still said to haunt the battlefield near the Hummelbaugh House.*

W. O. B. Branch    Earl Van Dorn    J. H. Morgan.    W. Barksdale

tossed into gaps in the rocks and covered with stones.

When the photographer Alexander Gardner and his colleagues arrived to photograph the scene, many of the dead had already been taken away, but enough were left to help him record Devil Den's "harvest of death," as he put it. His most famous photograph is of a

dead Confederate sharpshooter slumped behind a makeshift barricade of stones and boulders (see page 38). However, it was later claimed that he faked the shot, dragging the corpse of a Confederate soldier over to the spot and posing him for the camera. He added that he returned four months later and found that the soldier was still there. Faked or not,

*Above:* The immodest (and immoral) Major General "Fighting Joe" Hooker surveys the battlefield. He was relieved of command of the Army of the Potomac just a few days before Gettysburg.

this photograph has come to sum up the carnage of Devil's Den and remains one of the most poignant photographic images of the whole war. Another legacy of the fighting is the recurring instances of ghostly sightings in the mass of boulders or the slopes of Little Round Top beyond. The stories are too numerous to recount in detail, so a handful

of typical accounts will have to serve. One involves a female tourist who visited Devil's Den during the early 1970s.

She approached a park ranger and told him her story. She claimed that she was taking photographs on the edge of the jumble of boulders when she felt someone was standing beside her. She described the man as a scruffy "hippy" type, with bare feet and wearing a large shapeless hat. According to her story, the man looked at her and said, "What you are looking for is over there." With that he pointed behind her. She turned to look, but when she turned back the man had vanished. Had she seen a ghost pointing the way to his unmarked grave? A few months later, another visitor approached the park rangers and gave a similar description of a barefoot "hippy" with long hair and ragged clothing who appeared in a photograph but had not definitely been there when the shot was being taken. Over the past three decades, the figure has been seen several more times, and many visitors have taken him to be a reenactor. They were photographed standing next to him, but when the film was developed, the figure supposedly disappeared. Perhaps instant digital photography will confirm the existence of this ghostly soldier once and for all! In the triangular area in front of Devil's Den made by a fork in Plum Run, it has been claimed that cameras and film equipment malfunction regularly. I have been to the spot, and my camera survived to tell the tale. Other visitors report hearing the sounds of battle amid the rocks, but once again, millions of other visitors experienced no such thing. The people who give the local ghost tours seem to believe in such occurrences, but then again, if they didn't believe and admitted it, it wouldn't be smart marketing. Certainly Devil's Den is one of the most chilling spots on the Gettysburg battlefield. Perhaps some people are particularly attuned to such phenomena, like Mrs. Scoville at Antietam. They might experience things the rest of us could never imagine.

Other spots on the battlefield have also had their fair share of ghostly sightings. Over the years, the park rangers have received reports of a ghostly line of Confederate infantry advancing across the deadly open space in front of Cemetery Ridge, forever reenacting the doomed glory of Pickett's Charge. Down near Devil's Den, the sounds of fighting have been heard coming from the Peach Orchard and the Wheatfield. This was the area where Longstreet's men charged on their way toward Little Round Top and where the apparitions of soldiers have also been seen in the trees between the two fields.

The area near the Peach Orchard has been associated with a more specific ghost—that of Confederate Brigadier General William Barksdale, a highly respected officer who commanded a veteran Mississippi brigade during the attack. His men attacked the Union troops of Birney's Division at the Peach Orchard, and Barksdale called out to his men, "Advance, advance! Brave Mississippians, one more charge and the day is ours!" It was, and the position was taken. However, as the Confederate advance continued to Plum Run, Barksdale was shot by Union soldiers who were less than fifty yards

**Below:** *This rock pile in Devil's Den once formed the setting for Alexander Gardner's famous photograph of a dead Confederate sharpshooter slumped beside his rifle at the back of the makeshift trench (page 38). It still remains one of the most moving spots on the battlefield today.*

away, and he fell, mortally wounded. As he lay dying, he cried, "I am killed! Tell my wife and children that I died fighting at my post." It was a melodramatic farewell, but his men were inspired and drove the Union troops back toward Cemetery Ridge, so turning the flank of Sickles's corps and forcing it back onto Little Round Top. If Longstreet had any reserves, he could have turned the whole Union position, but by that stage no fresh troops were available, and the sacrifice of Barksdale and over seven hundred of his Mississippians proved vain. The dying general had to lie where he had fallen for several minutes, while fighting raged around him. One account by an officer from the 148th Pennsylvania Regiment claims that he saw Barksdale being fed water from a spoon by a young boy, presumably a drummer or runner. When the enemy was driven back, he was taken to the nearby Hummelbaugh House, where a casualty station had been set up, but it was too late—Barksdale died before he could be operated on. According to the stories, Barksdale's voice can still be heard crying out for water, the voice coming from the alleyway beside the house.

After the war, Mrs. Barksdale visited Gettysburg to exhume her husband's body and bring him back to his beloved Mississippi. She was accompanied by Barksdale's old dog, but when the animal reached the side of its master's grave, it lay down and began howling, refusing to stop or to move away. Throughout the exhumation, the dog remained by the graveside, even after Barksdale's body was removed from the grave and

taken away. Mrs. Barksdale had little choice but to leave the dog in the care of the homeowner. Over the next few weeks, the dog refused any food and water and eventually died at the side of its master's grave. The legend grew, and reportedly every July 2, you can hear the dog howling for its lost master. As a dog owner, I am hard-pressed to imagine a dog refusing food, but I can attest to the steadfast loyalty of man's best friend.

A few other houses around the battlefield have ghosts, many of them buildings that were turned into makeshift hospitals. Like so many historic buildings on Civil War battlefields, the suffering experienced there seems to have produced more accounts of ghosts than the scenes of the fighting itself. Is this because it is easier to imagine ghosts in old historic properties with a bloody past, or is there more to it than that? One of

*Above: Confederate prisoners captured at Gettysburg. The "hippy-like" figures described near Devil's Den were dressed in a similar manner to these men. Do ghosts still haunt the boulders below Little Round Top?*

*Above: The bodies of Confederate casualties await burial. The camera is looking toward the orchard on the haunted Rose Farm. In most armies, burial parties saw to their own dead first, so the dead of the losing side might lie around in the summer heat for several days before being laid to rest. The later reburial of bodies like these has also been surrounded by supernatural tales.*

these is the Rose Farm, whose grounds became a temporary cemetery after the fighting was over. Although the bodies were exhumed and moved four months later in November 1863, the process apparently proved too traumatic for a daughter of the farm owner, who went mad during the lengthy process of exhumation, identification, and reburial. She even claimed to see blood seeping through the outer walls of the farmhouse, although whether this was linked to the farm's service as a hospital or a cemetery is unclear. She simply saw too much of the horrors of sudden and gory death, and the evidence that literally lay all around her proved too much of a mental burden for her. One report from the 1920s from a man who participated in these exhumations mentions seeing strange blue lights floating around the Rose Farm, over the spots where the bodies had once been buried. Was that something he imagined, or were the lights linked to the souls of soldiers whose bodies were never exhumed?

Finally, there is the George Weikert Farm, now owned by the National Park Service. George and Ann Weikert left the house during the second day of the battle to escape the fighting, and their house was immediately turned into a casualty station. Over the years, several strange things have been reported in the house: doors that refuse to stay closed and the sound of pacing footsteps coming from an empty attic. These accounts are similar to those from other supposedly haunted houses, but like the Phillip Pry House at Antietam, these stories are made even more intriguing because the people who report them are often the park rangers themselves.

# Skirmishes with Ghosts

*"The hardships of forced marches are often more painful than the dangers of battle."*

GENERAL THOMAS "STONEWALL" JACKSON

The great battlefields of the war are not the only places have ghostly Civil War associations. Many smaller engagements or incidents in the war produced their share of unexplained events and strange apparitions. Whether there is any truth in them is almost impossible to judge. However, taken collectively, they amount to a substantial caucus of suggestive evidence that some supernatural force might indeed still linger in the odd corner of a long-forgotten battlefield or in a house where some dark wartime story unfolded. The following selection of stories is indicative of the many such tales in circulation.

Virginia's Shenandoah Valley was described as "the breadbasket of the Confederacy," and well into 1864, its farmers produced the food needed to keep Robert E. Lee's Army of Northern Virginia in the field. Many people have heard of Thomas "Stone-wall" Jackson's campaign in the Shenandoah Valley, a series of engagements and rapid marches that many military historians still deem a perfect example of how to wage war against a superior force. Jackson's "foot soldiers" out-marched and outfought several Union armies, and by the summer of 1862, they managed to clear the Shenandoah of the northern invaders. However, the Valley Army then marched east and joined Lee during the bitter fighting around Richmond known as the Seven Days Battles, then fought at Second Manassas, Antietam, and Fredericksburg. When the redoubtable Stonewall was killed in his moment of victory at Chancellorsville in May 1863, the Valley Army was amalgamated into the Army of Northern Virginia. Thomas Jackson's arm was amputated after the Battle of Chancellorsville and buried under a stone marker at the field hospital four miles from

*Inset: The dashing Confederate cavalry commander "Jeb" Stuart (1833–1864) might still be seen leading his men in his dramatic ride around the Union Army.*

*Below left: A Union courier reporting to General Sheridan during his vengeful campaign of 1864 in the Shenandoah Valley. The ghosts of the men he led may still linger in the lush valley they devastated on their march.*

*Below right: General Sheridan's Union Army of the Shenandoah, pictured on the march in pursuit of General Early's heavily outnumbered Confederates.*

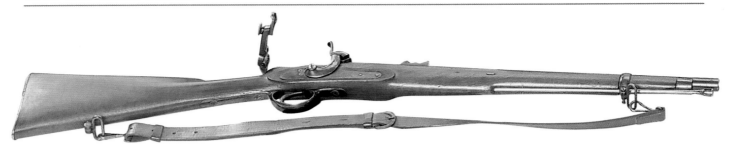

the battlefield. Jackson was moved south to convalesce, but his condition worsened and he died 125 miles away at Guinea Station on May 10.

Jackson was buried in Lexington, Virginia, but according to several ghost-story writers, both his grave and his deathbed are sometimes visited by the ghost of a weeping woman dressed in mourning black. Others claim that the amputated arm has even been seen over the grave, trying to rejoin the rest of the general's body!

After the defeat of Gettysburg, the valley lay open to a second Union invasion, and this time there was no Stonewall to keep the Union armies at bay. On May 15, 1864, General Breckenridge attacked and defeated a Union army at New Market, Virginia, the charge being led by the young cadets from the Virginia Military Institute, an academy still in existence today. According to legend, young soldiers can sometimes be seen on the battlefield and, on or around the anniversary of the battle, the sound of gunfire can be heard, as if the guns were firing far in the distance. Even more alarming, in May 1964 a group of tourists claim to have seen a reenactment of the charge of the cadets while they were having a picnic near the battlefield beside the old Route 11 (once the Valley Turnpike) on nearby Bushong's Hill. At first the onlookers assumed the young men were students at the Virginia Military Institute, practicing for some commemorative event. The cadet reenactors advanced, then when they reached the lower slopes of Bushong's Hill, they broke into a charge, passing the

picnickers and disappearing over the crest. It was only afterwards that the visitors realized that all the time the cadets had been in sight, they made no sound. On investigation, it was discovered there was no reenactment that day, leaving the visitors wondering what exactly they had witnessed.

While Lee and Grant fought a series of bloody and attritional battles in central Virginia—the Wilderness, Spotsylvania Courthouse, the North Anna River, and Cold Harbor—General Sheridan led an army of quite overwhelming force into the Shenandoah Valley, determined to deny Lee's army the food it needed to remain in the field. To this very day, the inhabitants of the valley still refer to the progress of his army as the "Burning."

*Above:* Jeb Stuart's carbine is typical of the weapons carried by the horsemen of either side, at least until the Union troopers began to be issued with repeating breech-loading carbines.

*Left:* General Sheridan pictured on his horse, Rienzi, riding into battle at Cedar's Creek. "Sheridan's Ride" began when he addressed his cavalrymen, exclaiming: "Boys, those of you who are not cowards follow me; for I'll sleep in that camp tonight or I'll sleep in Hell!" According to many inhabitants of the Shenandoah Valley, he well deserved such a fate.

*Previous page:* A makeshift dressing station for those wounded at the Battle of Gaines's Mill. The suffering of those damaged by the weapons of modern warfare—and the Civil War was most cartainly a "modern" war in this respect—is intensified by the relatively undeveloped state of medicine and surgery.

*Right:* General Philip H. Sheridan (1831–1888) distinguished himself at Murfreesboro, Chattanooga, and Chickamauga, but to most Virginians he is still remembered as the man who laid waste to the Shenandoah Valley during 1864 in much the same way as General Sherman did during his march from Atlanta to the sea later that same year.

On October 18, 1864, a Confederate force of 15,000 men under the command of General Early blocked Sheridan's way near the town of Middleton, Virginia. The Confederates were outnumbered two to one, but at dawn the following morning, Early launched his men into the attack, an assault that caught the Union army completely unawares. Three Confederate divisions swept through the enemy encampment, and by mid-morning it was all over, as the remains of Sheridan's army fled the field. Any pursuit proved impossible as the ragged and half-starved Confederate soldiers ransacked the well-stocked Union camp. This gave Sheridan the time he needed to rally his men north of Middleton, and at four in the afternoon, he launched a counterattack that broke the resistance of Early's Army of the Valley. When Sheridan launched Custer's cavalry at the retiring enemy, the retreat became a rout, and Confederate soldiers were cut down in their hundreds as they fled south. This engagement, known as the Battle of Cedar Creek, broke the back of Confederate resistance in the Shenandoah Valley. While the Union army lost some 5,665 men killed or seriously wounded that day, Early lost 3,000 men, losses the Confederate cause simply could not afford.

Union casualties were treated in casualty clearing stations set up in Middletown, most

*Above: Captain Orson H. Hart, the assistant adjutant general of the Army of the Potomac's III Corps pictured near Middleton, Virginia, in late 1863 or early 1864. It seems a ghostly rider still patrols the roads outside the town to this day.*

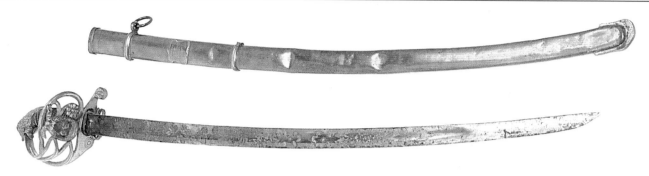

*Above: The Confederate cavalry saber of Brigadier General Archibald Gracie, who was killed at Petersburg in 1864. Personal possessions of the dead are often said to retain some link with their previous owners, and many weapons such as this have since been the subject of supernatural experiences for their new owners.*

in the local church. The dead were buried temporarily in the churchyard, and a few months later a Union burial detachment returned to Middletown to exhume the bodies and take them back north. It was then that the hauntings began.

At night, residents and soldiers alike would see a flickering blue light emerge from the church, then drift over to where the new coffins were laid out ready for shipment back home. Witnesses claim it looked like a candle, searching among the coffins as if looking for one in particular.

On another evening, a ghostly image appeared from the church, but this time it resembled an animal, either a small calf or a large dog, depending on which version of the tale you hear. These events stopped when the bodies were taken to the nearby railhead and began the long journey to their final places of rest.

Other strange events associated with the battle include the sounds of wounded and dying men coming from the fields between Middletown and Cedar Creek, roughly where the Union encampments were located. Gunfire can be heard rolling over the battlefield, much like it is said to do at New Market. Several buildings in Middletown or near the battlefield also claim to have resident ghosts. Middletown's Wayside Inn claims to be the oldest working inn in America and boasts a haunted room, number 14. Visitors say they have encountered either Union or Confederate soldiers in the downstairs lobby and have heard mysterious footsteps in the night. Close by, the Wayside Theatre claims to be

haunted by the ghost of a former caretaker who died in a fire, while the Belle Grove Plantation located next to the battlefield itself is supposedly haunted by a woman mourning her dead Confederate husband. She wears a black dress, her head is covered in a veil, and she can be seen looking out of an upper-floor window.

Whenever the room is inspected, it is always found to be empty, but its door refuses to stay closed. The house is also visited by a mystery horse-drawn carriage, which is heard pulling up to the front door but has never been seen.

On the roads leading south from the battlefield toward Cedar Creek, where Custer's cavalry cut down the fleeing Confederate soldiers, locals claim that phantom horses still ride, always coming from the north. Just when the startled listener thinks the horse is on top of them—the moment when a ghostly saber might swing down—the sound ceases.

In 1883, one man claims to have encountered a column of marching soldiers who marched straight past without looking at him. Then there is the tale of a local farmer, Holt Hottel, whose property lay on the southwestern corner of the battlefield. He claimed he came across a vagrant who refused to move from his barn. The farmer jabbed at him with a pitchfork, but the tool passed right through the figure. The farmer ran. Others claim to have seen the ghost of a scruffy-looking figure wearing what looks like the uniform of a Confederate soldier as he walked by the banks of the creek.

*Left: Confederate partisan leader John Singleton Mosby (1833–1916) operated in the Shenandoah Valley and northern Virginia, attacking Union supply trains and interdicting the enemy's lines of communication. To the Union soldiers who faced him, his men were little more than armed bandits.*

Finally, there is the ghostly band, which is said to play regimental airs from the Civil War, perpetually rehearsing inside Middletown's haunted church. Whatever the truth in all these tales, it is clear that Middletown, Virginia, and the battlefield outside the small town remains one of the most celebrated haunting areas in the Shenandoah.

Lee used the Shenandoah as a springboard for his invasion of Maryland in 1862, and while a part of his army laid siege to and captured Harpers Ferry, the rest of his army was scattered across the Maryland countryside. During the campaign, Confederate blocking forces tried to stop the advance of the leading elements of General McClellan's

HARPER'S WEEKLY.
JOURNAL OF CIVILIZATION

Vol. VII.—No. 349.]     NEW YORK, SATURDAY, SEPTEMBER 5, 1863.

*Right: Mosby's men capture a Union sutler's wagon. The ghosts of a handful of his troopers are still said to haunt the Shenandoah, and the inexplicable supernatural being—dubbed the "Whirlaway" by those who encountered it near Front Royal, Virginia—is said to be the vengeful spirit of one of Mosby's partisans.*

Army of the Potomac at South Mountain, buying time for Lee to gather his army together at Sharpsburg. On September 14, three separate engagements were fought on South Mountain, but it was only in the south at Crampton's Gap that the attackers managed to break through the Confederate defenses and gain a passage through the mountains for the rest of the Union army.

The wounded were taken to the nearby towns of Bolivar or Burkittsville, Maryland, where almost every house was filled with soldiers or turned into a makeshift casualty station.

Another well-known account of a Shenandoah ghost involved the Confederate guerilla band commanded by Colonel John Mosby. His partisan cavalry operated throughout northern Virginia, tearing up railroad tracks, ambushing Union supply convoys, and generally making life difficult for the enemy on Virginian soil.

When Sheridan launched his invasion of the Shenandoah Valley in the late summer of 1864, Mosby's raiders began harassing his supply columns, playing a cat-and-mouse game with the vastly more numerous force of Union cavalry attached to Sheridan's army. The fighting became increasingly bitter, and at one stage the Union troopers captured six of Mosby's men. Most of his partisans came from the Shenandoah, so to make a point, the prisoners were taken to Front Royal, Virginia, where two were hanged and the remaining four were shot.

In retaliation, Mosby's men executed three Union prisoners, and the Union army decided to avoid any more summary executions. However, it seems the spirits of the executed men never left the town. Six years later, in 1870, a resident of Front Royal was taken aback when a sudden blast of whirling wind ripped past him. He then saw a shimmering light, which slowly transformed itself into the image of a Confederate soldier or partisan. His flickering image seemed to accompany the rushing wind and whirled back and forth before disappearing into the night. The locals immediately dubbed this phantom image the "Whirlaway." It seemed to reappear every six years, and on some occasions, the residents of Front Royal felt threatened by the apparition. Around 1906, a local judge met the being and recounted that it terrified him, but that it soon disappeared out of sight.

In 1925, a Mrs. Cook and her daughters encountered the Whirlaway in their garden, accompanied by the sound of footsteps on the path leading to their house. They fled inside, and they later told the local paper that the phantom moved extremely quickly but remained swirling around their house for most of the rest of the day.

According to local legend, the Whirlaway is the ghost of a young man from Front Royal who either wanted to join Mosby's raiders but was killed by Union troops before he could, or alternatively, the specter belongs to one of the partisans executed in the town by Sheridan's men in 1864. Whatever the cause of the phenomenon, many current residents of Front Royal believe that the Whirlaway is still out there, waiting to pay them a visit.

Today, the hill where the road runs through the Crampton's Gap battlefield is know as "Spook Hill." According to local legend, if someone stops their car and puts it into neutral at the bottom of the slope near Burkittsville, then the driver will sometimes feel the car being pushed back up the hill to the summit. The car is pushed by ghosts, those of the men who manhandled an artillery piece up the same hill in September 1862 during the fighting there.

Other residents claim that on some nights they can see campfires flickering on the hills above Crampton's Gap and Fox's Gap to the north, the ghostly reminders of the passage of two great armies almost 150 years ago. Some claim to have approached the fires, only to find they extinguished as they moved close to them, leaving no trace of burning behind. Others say they have seen the ghosts of soldiers warming themselves beside these fires or lying asleep around the fire.

Another area with its fair share of Civil War ghosts is the Tidewater region in Virginia, where General McClellan launched his abortive Peninsula Campaign in the spring of 1862 and where Lee defeated the Army of the Potomac in a string of hard-fought and bloody engagements known as the Seven Days Battles. The Union army marched through the area again in the summer of 1864, and after Grant suffered a serious reverse at Cold Harbor, he moved his army across the James River and laid siege to Petersburg, Virginia.

*Above:* The swampy waters of the Chickahominy River, over which Jeb Stuart's men threw a bridge to aid their escape from the pursuing enemy in 1862. Did a modern Virginian encounter the general and his men repeating their exploit in the mid-twentieth century?

*Right:* The burial of Captain William D. Latané, the only Confederate cavalryman killed during Jeb Stuart's ride around the Union Army in front of Richmond in June 1862. Over a century later, a descendant of the dead officer claims he witnessed the death of his ancestor, who left behind a blood-soaked memento for posterity or even specifically for his great-grandson.

One of the most dramatic events of the Peninsular Campaign in 1862 was Jeb Stuart's ride around the Union army on June 12–15, when his Confederate horsemen demonstrated to Lee that the disposition of McClellan's army invited a massed attack on the Union right flank. The ride was certainly a dramatic and daring event that caught the public imagination, even more so because Stuart achieved this feat with the loss of only one man.

On June 13, 1862, some 1,200 Confederate horsemen road southeast from Hanover Court House to join the Studley Road, then they continued along it towards Old Church, a mile beyond Totopotomoy Creek. The few enemy pickets they encountered were easily bypassed or silenced, and when Stuart arrived at the creek, he found the small bridge was intact and undefended.

A mile beyond the creek at Linney Corner, they encountered a Union patrol, so a group of Confederate horsemen detached themselves from the main force to deal with them. In the short cavalry fight that followed, the two detachment commanders, Captain William Latané of the 9th Virginia Cavalry and Captain William Royall of the 5th U.S. Cavalry singled each other out for a personal duel. Although Latané wounded his opponent, Royall managed to fire two pistol shots at the Confederate officer, killing him instantly. The fight was over in seconds, and Royall and the surviving Union horsemen escaped towards Old Church, pursued by the rest of Latané's men. The young officer was the only Confederate casualty of the whole spectacular "ride."

After that, the Confederate horsemen fell on the Union rail depot at Tunstall's Station before continuing on to the south, laden with plunder and escorting some valuable

prisoners. Somehow, Stuart's men evaded the Union troops sent to corner them, and by dawn the next day the exhausted riders stood on the banks of the Chickahominy River.

The Forge Bridge had been destroyed, so they used timber from a nearby barn to repair the burned-out bridge. At one in the afternoon, the work was finished, and Stuart ordered his men across the river. They destroyed the bridge behind them just as Union cavalry patrols reached the far bank. Stuart and his men had evaded the enemy and continued their ride back to Richmond without any further difficulty.

On June 13, 1976, a group of Virginians were picnicking near the banks of Totopotomoy Creek, to the northeast of Richmond. They considered swimming in the river, but recent rains had made the water too fast-flowing, so they contented themselves with relaxing by its bank. They knew enough about Civil War history to realize they were close to the spot where Stuart's men crossed the creek during "Stuart's Ride." The picnickers included another William Latané, a medical student and the great-grandson of the Confederate officer killed at Linney Corner.

*Above: Artillery batteries at the Battle of Cold Harbor, June 3, 1864. Grant's attack proved a costly blunder; his army suffered 7,000 casualties in a single hour in front of the Confederate guns. It is said the ghosts of some of these poor men still linger on the once blood-soaked battlefield.*

When the picnic ended, the group returned to Richmond, although one of the party, Ed Farley, decided to take one of the two cars and explore the route taken by Stuart's cavalry. Of the group, he was the one who was most interested in Civil War history, and he hoped to find a trace of the old bridge where Stuart's men crossed the Chickahominy River on June 14, 1862. After all, one of his ancestors had ridden with Stuart that day. He drove the eight miles down Old Church road to Tunstall's Station, then took State Road 155 south for another ten miles or so until he reached Providence Forge, on Route 60. Three-quarters of a mile

farther on, he reached the Chickahominy, where he parked the car and began exploring.

It was a warm day, and he reckoned he must have dozed off for a short while. When he woke, he heard the sound of hammers striking wood a short distance away, accompanied by voices. He then saw a figure sleeping on the ground close by, dressed in the uniform of a Confederate cavalry officer. Thinking he must be a reenactor, he tapped him on the shoulder, and the figure stirred, then smiled, and told him not to worry. He added: "My cavalry will get the bridge built in time, for if they don't we'll have plenty of excitement when the Yankees catch up with us." Farley was stunned.

The figure seemed to be a living reincarnation of Jeb Stuart! He backed away, heading towards the sound of the building work. Suddenly the sounds faded, and reluctant to retrace his steps, he headed for the safety of his car.

He wasn't the only person to see something that day. When William Latané and his two young women passengers left the picnic area, they took the River Road to Route 360, the main road heading towards Richmond, and drove down it about a mile and a half before they found the road was blocked at a crossroads by a mass of cavalry crossing Route 360 on Studley Road. They pulled over and stood beside the car to watch the show. They were amazed at how realistic the soldiers looked, particularly the impressive, dashing fellow playing the part of Jeb Stuart, who looked just like the old pictures of the general. They also noted the standard of horsemanship was superb, but as they watched, the horsemen broke into a canter, heading towards a group of horsemen in the distance on the left, dressed as Union troops.

The two groups of horsemen clashed, and as they did, one of the Confederate riders fell. As his companions picked him up, the rest drove the enemy out of sight, and the sound of the riders and the reenactment faded into the distance.

When they got home, they decided to inquire into the event and were told that no reenactment had been scheduled that day, let alone one involving hundreds of riders. Had they seen the ghosts of Stuart's cavalry, and had William Latané watched the death of his ancestor on the same spot as more than a century before?

Latané has good reason to believe what he saw was genuine. After the riders passed, he noticed a scrap of cloth on the ground, which turned out to be the part of a silk handkerchief with his initials, W.L., embroidered into it. As he held it, he noticed it was spotted with fresh blood. Deciding to keep this bizarre find a secret, he later had it examined by a museum. It proved to be a genuine artifact from the Civil War era.

Both Latané and Farley remain convinced that what they saw that day was the ghostly passage of Stuart and his horsemen, and somehow the dead captain had reached back through time to leave a keepsake for his descendant.

I have heard two or three different versions of this tale, both of which have confused the history and geography behind it. The version given here has been adapted from the one given by the North Carolina historian Nancy Roberts in her book *Civil War Ghosts and Legends*. Despite my best efforts I have been unable to locate the two men involved in the story. While I would be loath to doubt their version of events, it would be better still if this incredible tale could be verified.

A short distance from the sites mentioned here is Cold Harbor, where in June 1864, Grant launched a disastrous assault on Lee's entrenched army, resulting in a battle that cost the lives of 7,000 men within an hour.

*Opposite: Burial parties recovering the dead from the battlefield of Cold Harbor in April 1865, some ten months after the battle. Photographs such as these managed to sum up the wasteful carnage of the attritional battles fought in Virginia during the last year of the war.*

During the two weeks the armies remained there, some 50,000 Union and 30,000 Confederate soldiers became casualties, making it one of the most brutal attritional battles of the war. Poignant photographs of burial parties recovering the bones of the fallen after the battle at Cold Harbor are probably as widely known as the one taken at Devil's Den. Like the neighboring battlefield of Gaines's Mill where Lee's army won a Pyrrhic victory over McClellan in May 1862, the site has a reputation for ghosts and strange experiences. Lights have been seen dancing in the trees in both places, and on Boatswain's Creek on the Gaines's Mill battlefield, the ghosts of soldiers have been spotted briefly before they vanished.

One interesting experience by a visitor to the Cold Harbor battlefield involved little more than an unspoken name. He and his wife decided to follow the National Park Service battlefield trail at Cold Harbor, which took them across the field where Grant's men made their fatal charge and then into the woods where the remains of entrenchments can still be seen on either side of the path. He describes a kind of guide:

In certain areas, the sense of sorrow is almost overwhelming. As we were walking, I just knew that we were not alone. At one of the rifle pits, I had the sense of a very young man there, in his late teens, and the name that came into my mind was Joshua. As we walked away, I felt as if this young man was still walking with us, almost like we were being escorted away. After we had cleared the rifle pit and gained the top of the hill, this feeling fell away. After we left the battlefield area, we went to the cemetery and started looking for some of the names that we had sensed in their records. Oddly enough, there was only one Joshua out of over 900 names recorded in the records, and he was marked as being a part of an infantry unit. While this may be coincidence or not, I know what I felt and experienced that day.

The feeling of oppressiveness in places that have seen such a bloody historical event is not an unusual one, but the feeling that someone was trying to contact the living is much rarer. Although thousands of people walk that same path every year, it seems as if only a few are attuned enough to hear such "voices" or even to see certain sights that the rest of us remain ignorant of.

There are many other examples of Civil War ghosts, such as the report of a woman calling out for a missing husband or son named Jacob at the Wilderness, or the sight of soldiers crossing Cobblestone Bridge near the site of First Manassas. Together they would fill several volumes like this. What is clear is that in certain places where certain historical events took place, some but not all the people who pass through that spot are susceptible to feelings or encounters that are difficult to describe and even harder to substantiate. If ghosts really do exist, it is unsurprising that they would appear in places where so much human suffering has been concentrated, as described by Hermann Melville so memorably in his poem on the Wilderness:

Green shoes full of bones, the mouldering coat
And cuddled up skeleton;
And scores of such. Some start as in dreams,
And comrades lost bemoan.

*Above: A selection of Confederate artifacts recovered from the battlefields of Virginia, including the metal remains of rifled muskets, knives, swords, buckles, and even a tin canteen found beside Totopotomy Creek, close to the spot where Captain Latané fell in May 1862.*

*Opposite: Grant's chief of staff, Major General John A. Rawlin, was unhorsed at Cold Harbor, and the animal fell into Confederate hands. The equine POW was photographed. It was through Rawlin's intervention that Grant, a recovering alcoholic, avoided the temptation to seek solace in whiskey after the defeat.*

# GHOSTS
# OF THE WEST

UNLIKE THE CAMPAIGN IN THE EAST, where the fighting was
concentrated in a relatively small area, the war in the
western theater was spread over half a continent, with the
heaviest fighting taking place in Kentucky, Tennessee, and
Mississippi. The Union grand strategy to defeat the
Confederacy involved a maritime blockade of the southern
coastline linked to a drive down the Mississippi River. With
the Mississippi in Union hands, the Confederacy would be
cut in two, leaving Texas, Arkansas, and most of Louisiana
isolated from the Confederate heartland. The ultimate prize
would be the Mississippi River fortress of Vicksburg, and
with that in Union hands, the invading armies could march
wherever they wanted. The west had its share of great
battlefields, but unlike the often open agricultural
battlefields of the east, these engagements were sometimes
fought in dense woods, where it was difficult to determine
where the enemy was or which way led to safety in case of
defeat. When the battle was over, it proved equally difficult
to recover casualties. Many remained where they had fallen
for months or even years. These aspects of the western
campaign are reflected in the ghost tales associated with it.
There are similarities to some of the tales from the east,
showing that ghosts, or ghost stories, are not sharply
differentiated by region.

*Left: One of the most phtographed battle sites for obvious reasons,
Lookoout Mountain was stormed by General Hooker's men in
November 1863 and taken from the Confederates despite the
daunting height of 1,100 feet.*

# Ghosts of Shiloh

*"War is cruelty. There's no use trying to reform it,
the crueler it is the sooner it will be over."*

GENERAL WILLIAM TECUMSEH SHERMAN

The Union campaign in the West began in earnest in February 1862, when a largely unknown commander, Brigadier General Ulysses S. Grant, captured the Confederate strongholds of Fort Henry and Fort Donelson, which guarded against an advance down the Cumberland and Tennessee Rivers southward past the Tennessee state line. This meant that Tennessee lay wide open to attack, so the Confederates were forced to retreat south out of Kentucky and even to give up Nashville, Tennessee. They regrouped in Corinth, Mississippi. Meanwhile, a newly promoted Grant transported his 40,000-strong army down the Tennessee River to Pittsburgh Landing, some fifteen miles northeast of Corinth, where he hoped to join forces with another Union army of 55,000 men that was then in Nashville. Unfortunately for Grant, the Confederate commander Albert S. Johnston mobilized his army before Buell's Union Army could reach the Tennessee River,

*Below: The Battle of Shiloh was the first full battle in the western theater, and as a reminder of its horror, the ghosts of those who fell are still said to haunt the woods around Pittsburgh Landing.*

*Right:* General William T. Sherman's division bore the brunt of the first Confederate attacks near Shiloh Church, but after an initial withdrawal, his men stood firm despite suffering heavy casualties. The dead were later buried in the woods surrounding the church.

and on April 6, 1862, he launched an all-out assault on Grant's forward divisions encamped near Shiloh Church. The Union line was forced back in disorder, but the confused fighting in the woods left the Confederates as disorientated as their retreating enemy. This confusion was increased when Johnston was killed, and dogged groups of Union defenders were able to regroup and hold on in a position that became known as the "Hornets Nest," protected by a sunken road that was turned into a makeshift trench by defenders. Eventually the Confederates forced the Union troops back from the sunken road and the nearby Peach Orchard, and as darkness fell, Grant's line had been thrown back almost to Pittsburgh Landing, with its back to the river. Disaster was only averted by the fire support of Union gunboats on the Tennessee River and by the fall of darkness.

During the night, General Buell's 55,000 reinforcements began to arrive. The following morning, the Confederates planned to renew the attack, but it was the reinvigorated Union army that struck first. It outnumbered the battered Confederate army by two to one, and the outcome of the second phase was never in doubt. By early afternoon, the Confederate Army of the Mississippi was in full retreat, leaving almost 10,000 of its men behind as casualties, either killed, wounded, or missing. Although Grant's army suffered a similar number of casualties, they held the field and managed to unite their two armies on the Mississippi border.

One of the most commonly reported ghost stories concerning the battle is that of

the "Phantom Drummer," whose drumming can still be heard in the vicinity of Shiloh Church around the anniversary of the battle. Visitors have complimented the park rangers on providing such an atmospheric backdrop for the battlefield tours, only to be told that no drummer was hired. Unlike many reported ghosts, that of the Phantom Drummer remains invisible, and only his persistent and melancholy beating can be heard. According to tradition, the drummer was a mere boy, serving in a Union regiment attached to Don Carlos Buell's army, which force-marched to the Tennessee River to save Grant's troops from destruction. The drummer's regiment took part in the Union assault on the second

*Above: This bullet-splintered stump of a tree near the Peach Orchard marks the spot where the Confederate commander fell during the climax of the Battle of Shiloh.*

*Opposite: A 12-pounder Napoleon smoothbore artillery piece stands guard over Fort Donelson, where the ghosts of the dead are said to disturb residents in the Crowe House, a wartime hospital.*

*Right: General Albert S. Johnston (1802–1862) was wounded in the leg during the battle but ignored the wound and bled to death. His body was taken to New Orleans for burial but was later reinterred in Austin, Texas. He was one of almost 25,000 men who became casualties during the two-day battle.*

day of the fighting, and as the story goes, the troops soon came under extremely heavy fire from a well-defended Confederate position. The Colonel ordered the drummer to sound the retreat, but after a pause the boy began beating the signal for the attack. When the officer rounded on the boy, he was told, "But, Sir! 'Attack' is all I know! I never learned 'Retreat'!" The boy's lack of training resulted in his regiment rising up and charging the enemy, and after a short but hard-fought struggle, they broke the Confederate line. Afterwards, they found the dead body of the drummer boy, shot through the heart in the closing minutes of the fight. It would be all too easy to dismiss this melodramatic story for fiction or at least see it as an apocryphal

story conjured up to summarize the battle that day. However, in the late-1940s a new road was being built through the battlefield, and the construction team unearthed several bodies, one of which was that of a young drummer boy aged about fourteen, with traces of his drum cord still looped around his neck. A bullet lay in his chest cavity, where his heart would have been.

Other sounds that have been heard in various parts of the battlefield are those of men marching close to Pittsburgh Landing or the sounds of wounded men crying out for help or water near the Shiloh Church, and a few visitors have expressed their unease and a feeling of intense cold while walking around the Hornet's Nest.

Like the battlefields in the East, these sounds or feelings tend to be experienced in places where the fighting was most intense.

The discovery of unmarked graves during the road construction would have come as little surprise to the park rangers at Shiloh National Battlefield Park, as the confused nature of the terrain, with its dense wood thickets and small ravines, meant that many bodies were missed by the burial parties and were either buried where they lay some time later or else remained unburied until the bodies decayed sufficiently to blend in with the forest floor. According to one park ranger, the dispersed bodies also meant that Civil War artifacts were scattered across the battlefield and so were relatively easy prey to grave robbers equipped with metal detectors. These men would turn up at night and scour some of the remote corners of Shiloh battlefield, hoping to find a contact that might turn out to be a valuable belt buckle, a row of buttons, or a bayonet.

One man in particular was reputed to have visited the battlefield at night over the

*Above: This pond marks the eastern end of the sunken road, which formed the main defensive position in Shiloh's "Hornet's Nest." Some visitors claim the area around the pond seems intensely cold, even in the heat of summer.*

space of several years, and he proved particularly adept at finding objects to sell to unscrupulous collectors. The park rangers never managed to catch him with looted artifacts or digging up an unmarked grave site.

One night, park rangers were patrolling through the woods to the northwest of Shiloh Church when they found a metal detector lying on the ground—brand-new, but accidentally broken. A little farther on, where a track wound through the trees, they came upon a car with the owner of the metal detector sitting inside it. When the rangers approached, they found he was paralyzed by fear and seemed to have experienced some kind of severe trauma. He was taken to the Corinth Hospital, where he was treated and then released into psychiatric care. He never fully recovered and never spoke of what happened to him that night in the woods. The rumors soon spread, though, the most persistent one being that he had been digging in a spot his detector suggested a metal artifact might be when he unearthed a row of buttons from a soldier's tunic. As he knelt down to pick them up, a skeletal hand rose from the earth and grabbed them back again! While this is pretty far-fetched, something or someone did make the grave robber lose his sanity in the Shiloh woods.

The park rangers never found any signs of a disturbed grave site when they inspected the area the following day. Had he disturbed the resting place of the ghost of a fallen soldier and the specter turned on him, or was

there a more rational explanation? While the true facts may never be known, the story of the man's encounter certainly deterred other metal detector–owners from following in the man's footsteps. Possibly the ghosts of Shiloh were indeed successful in protecting their own graves.

Before leaving Shiloh, it is worth recounting the story of Mrs. Ann Wallace, the wife of one of Grant's divisional commanders, Brigadier General William H. L. Wallace (not to be confused with fellow divisional commander Brigadier General Lew Wallace, who later wrote *Ben Hur*). Wallace had posted his troops between Shiloh Church and the Tennessee River, which put his men in the front line when the Confederates launched their attack. It was his men who defended the Peach Orchard and the sunken road and who created the defensive position known as the Hornet's Nest.

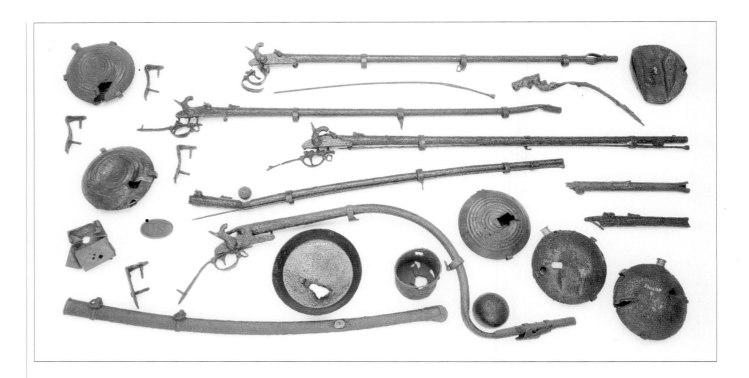

When the Union line finally broke, the Confederates poured through the defenses, and as Wallace tried to rally his men, he was shot in the left eye by a musket ball and fell from his horse. The fire was too heavy for his staff to retrieve the body, so he was left behind when his men fled the field.

Meanwhile, his wife Anne was approaching Pittsburg Landing, having left her home in Ottawa, Illinois, a week before. Since her husband had marched away, she had been overcome by a feeling of foreboding and impending doom. By the last day in March, it had become overwhelming, so she decided to visit her husband. She took passage by riverboat down the Illinois and Mississippi Rivers to Cairo, Illinois, then joined an Illinois civilian delegation for the passage up the Tennessee to Pittsburg Landing. She arrived as the first day of battle was at its height, probably around the same time her husband was shot. She spent the night on the eastern bank with General Buell's staff, then crossed the following morning to tend the wounded as the army counterattacked. The Union troops recovered the ground where

Wallace had fallen, and they found her husband wrapped in a blanket supplied by a well-meaning Confederate soldier. He was extremely weak and sodden with the night's rain but still alive. The soldiers carried him to a hospital boat on the river, where his wife joined him. She later said, "Will recognized my voice right off and clasped my hand. I had believed him dead! And he was alive! And he knows me!" It was a moving reunion, but it was short-lived.

Wallace was taken to Grant's headquarters in Savannah, Tennessee, where his wife kept a vigil at her husband's bedside. However, his wound soon became infected, and as his wife put it, "He faded away like a fire going out." His last words were to his wife, waving her away when she seemed ready to weep with the words, "We meet in heaven." Wallace died on April 10. His wife took his body home and buried him in Ottawa, where to honor his memory, she commissioned a rather bizarre and macabre scene, with the general's horse, a national flag, and the general's portrait arranged outside the porch of the family home. According to the story, you

*Below: By the end of the first day of the battle, Pittsburgh Landing on the Tennessee River (where Anne Wallace had debarked) was thronged by Union troops who had fled but could run no farther.*

can still see the figure of Ann Wallace standing by the window of the Cherry House where her husband died, while another account tells of the ghost of a man looking out from an upstairs bedroom window. The figure is reportedly dressed in a broad-brimmed black hat but wears the uniform of a Union general. Are these the ghosts of the

Wallaces, or did some other unrecorded trauma take place in the same house?

If the story of Anne Wallace's prescient feelings in Ottawa about her husband's fate were not strange enough, the possibility that her ghost still remains by her husband's side goes much further into the realms of the unknown and unprovable.

# Ghosts of Murfreesboro

*"Rosencrans awoke General Thomas and said: 'Will you protect the rear on retreat to Overall's Creek?' Thomas promptly answered: 'This army can't retreat,' and then fell asleep again."*
THE LIFE OF MAJOR GENERAL GEORGE H. THOMAS, *THOMAS VAN HORNE, 1882*

After Shiloh, the war in the West resembled two distinct campaigns, one fought for control of the Mississippi and the other, which was probably of less strategic importance, for control of Tennessee. While Nashville had been occupied by Buell's Army of the Ohio as it marched on Shiloh, the country was far from secure. Consequently, Buell marched east from Corinth toward Chattanooga, hoping to sever Confederate rail links with the eastern half of the state. Over to the west, Confederate General Smith marched north from Knoxville, Tennessee, to challenge Union control of Kentucky, while General Bragg marched north from Chattanooga in support of Smith. The two armies joined forces at Perryville in October, just in time for Buell to appear and force them to battle. Bragg lost the fight and led his combined army back to Knoxville. He tried again, this time striking toward Nashville. By then, Buell had been replaced by Rosencrans and the force had been renamed the Army of the Cumberland.

*Below: The Battle of Murfreesboro, or Stone's River, as depicted in a contemporary watercolor engraving. The Confederate attackers are seen breaking against a solid line of Union troops during the second day of the fighting.*

*Right: General Braxton Bragg (1817–1876) was a cautious (and unpopular) commander who developed a reputation for retreating, but at Murfreesboro he launched his Army of the Tennessee into two furious but ultimately unsuccessful assaults against the Union line.*

*Left: The broken remains of two Union rifled artillery pieces litter the battlefield of Murfreesboro in this evocative but staged photograph. These woods near the Wilkinson Turn-pike are now regarded as a ghostly hot spot.*

*Right: On January 2, 1863, Bragg ordered his men to attack across the Stones River near this spot—directly into the line of Union men and guns waiting for them on the western bank. The area is now said to be haunted by the ghosts of those brave Southerners.*

Rosencrans marched to stop the Confederate drive, and this time Bragg's Army of the Tennessee and Rosencrans's Army of the Cumberland clashed outside Murfreesboro, some thirty-five miles southeast of Nashville. The Battle of Murfreesboro (also known as the Battle of Stones River) was a two-round affair that began on December 13, 1862, when Bragg launched an all-out attack on Rosencrans's line a few miles northwest of the town itself. At first the attack went well, with Hardee's Division driving in the Union flank and causing half the Union army to flee in panic. It was like a door swinging on its hinge, and the Union line was turned around ninety degrees to form a right angle. Somehow, Rosencrans rallied his men, and a new line was formed, buying time for troops to be move to the most threatened sectors of the battlefield.

Despite the stiffening resistance, the Confederate attacks continued, Bragg throwing men away in an attempt to break the reformed Union line and regain the victory that had been within his grasp. As night fell, the battle drew to a close, and both sides pulled back slightly and dug in. The fighting was renewed two days later, after a shocked lull that lasted all of New Year's Day, when both sides gathered their wounded from the field and tried to reorganize their shattered units. On the morning of January 2, 1863, Bragg launched General Breckenridge's division in an assault across Stones River, which fell upon the weakly held Union right wing. It was a bad blunder, as the Confederates were exposed to massed artillery fire as they waded the freezing river and Rosencrans had time to reinforce his line. The assault was stopped, and then a Union counterattack drove Breckenridge back across the river.

Unable to make any impression on the strengthened Union position, Bragg ordered a retreat, and the army pulled back thirty miles. For the next six months, the two armies remained facing each other without either commander making a move, and Bragg became the most castigated general in the Confederacy. His men quipped that it didn't matter if he won or lost, he would still retreat after a battle. Fortunately, the Army of the Cumberland was even more battered than the Confederate force, and at least Bragg had bought time for the ailing Confederate cause. Murfreesboro proved costly in terms of human lives for a battle with little strategic gain. Both sides lost around 9,000 men—killed, wounded, or missing—during the two days of fighting, and eyewitnesses describe how the bodies lay so close to each other that one could walk for a mile on them without touching the blood-caked frozen ground. Inevitably for a place that saw so many young men killed, the years that followed produced

*Left: A monument to the fallen was erected in the months following the Battle of Murfreesboro. Approximately 13,000 men fell on each side during the two days of battle, and the ghost of at least one of these men has been seen by reenactors in the vicinity of the monument. Were the spirits of the dead confused by the sight of modern-day soldiers walking over the ground where they fell?*

several instances where the ghosts of the soldiers came back to haunt the living.

Today, the Murfreesboro National Battlefield Park on the western edge of the city provides visitors with the opportunity to visit the principal sites of the battle, with walking and driving tours covering the con-tested ground. One of the more popular stops on the tour is "Slaughter Pen," where the center of the Union line held its ground and provided an anchoring point for the broken right wing of the army. The section of the Union line held by General Sheridan's Division formed the new apex of the Union

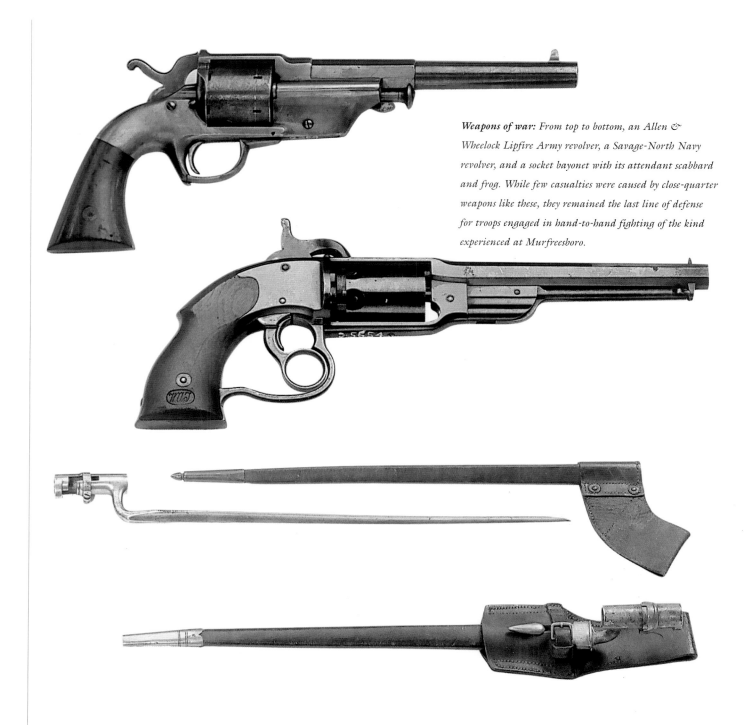

**Weapons of war:** *From top to bottom, an Allen & Wheelock Lipfire Army revolver, a Savage-North Navy revolver, and a socket bayonet with its attendant scabbard and frog. While few casualties were caused by close-quarter weapons like these, they remained the last line of defense for troops engaged in hand-to-hand fighting of the kind experienced at Murfreesboro.*

line, and it soon became the target of a series of fierce but ultimately unsuccessful Confederate attacks. Although the defenders were driven back almost half a mile and Sheridan lost a third of his division, the line held firm. At times, the men fought hand-to-hand, using bayonets, knives, and even teeth. It was a brutal affair and a costly one, earning that patch of wooded ground the name "Slaughter Pen."

Some visitors to the site often report a stillness in the air, as if the ground is somehow hallowed and special. Sometimes a complete silence in the woods seems to descend, the sounds of traffic or activity in the background fading away, leaving visitors with a

*The revolver at the top, the imported Le Mat, was a masterpiece in firearm design and a prized possession. It was the chosen weapon of Confederate cavalryman Jeb Stuart, whose ghostly image has reportedly been seen beside Virginia's Chickahominy River. Below it is a Confederate Columbus Firearms Company version of a Colt Navy revolver. Below are a side knife and a "Bowie" bayonet.*

growing sense of foreboding. Park rangers have also noticed that it often seems much colder around Slaughter Pen than elsewhere on the battlefield. Some reenactors who have spent the night camped on the site of Slaughter Pen have reported that they felt they were not alone, and that the spirits of the dead were watching them. A few of these modern reenactors went further, claiming to have seen the figure of a soldier on the periphery of their living history encampment, or just outside the circle of light cast by their campfire. Other visitors have also described encounters with the mysterious figure, almost always accompanied by the same feeling that something not quite human is close by.

*Left: Major General William Hardee (1815–1873) wrote a book about infantry tactics before the war, then put his teachings into practice at Shiloh, Perryville, Chattanooga, Atlanta, and Bentonville. He was known as the "Gray Ghost," a title that referred to his ability to outflank and outmarch his opponents, not any supernatural trait.*

He has been seen standing in the trees, or even within plain view in the open, as if wanting to join the living but unable to do so. If anyone calls out to him or tries to approach him, the figure disappears. A few felt they were being followed and heard the sounds of movement behind them. When they turned around, there was nobody there.

Reenactors who have camped in the area at night have also mentioned seeing bluish lights moving through the trees, seeming to wax and wane for a few seconds or even min-

MAJ. GEN. WILLIAM S. ROSECRANS.
AT THE BATTLE OF MURFREESBORO, JANY 2ND 1862.

*Above: General Rosen-crans's Army of the Cumberland took months to recover from its "victory" at Murfreesboro, and after the bloodbath of "Slaughter Pen," his men lost much of their faith in their commander. Before his death in 1898, he claimed to be haunted by the images of the men he had lost at Murfreesboro.*

utes before fading away completely. While some of this could be explained away by the heightened awareness of modern Civil War, for reenactors in a place that has seen so much bloodshed, the uneasy feeling remains that something or someone might be out there, still haunting the trees around Slaughter Pen and attracted by the sense of lost comradeship that the reenactors seem to offer him.

In 1978, the ghost-story writer Richard Winer interviewed Jeffrey Leathers, a park ranger who often participated in reenactment events at Murfreesboro and other battlefields. According to the account, Mr. Leathers was

camping on the battlefield with other reenactors near McFadden's Ford where Breckenridge's attack was launched on January 2, 1862. Leathers woke up in the middle of the night, and discovering he was thirsty, he collected his reproduction canteen, rose, and walked towards the Park Service administration building a half mile away, where he planned to fill it. He noticed someone hiding in the bushes beside the path, and thinking he was a fellow reenactor planning to surprise him, Leathers called out to the figure to show himself. Both Leathers and the figure were in period costume, and as the man rose from hiding and approached him with one palm raised as a token of surrender, Leathers thought he was playacting.

He called out to the man to halt, then raised his musket and pointed it at the stranger, just like a real sentry would have done. The man dropped to the ground, then seemed to vanish in the dark shadows. Still thinking a trick was being played on him, Leathers explored the bushes but found no sign of the man. The next morning he returned to the spot, but apart from his own footprints, he found no trace of the soldier he had challenged the night before. He then began to remember hearing of the ghostly figures of soldiers prowling the battlefield and hovering around reenactors. Could he have been duped by a fellow reenactor, or was the man he encountered the ghost of a Civil War soldier, confused by the familiar sights the reenactors conjured up for him and trying to find a way to join the men he presumed were his long-lost comrades?

# Ghosts of Lower Mississippi

*"After the battle . . . one is naturally disposed to do as much
to alleviate the suffering of an enemy as a friend."*
ULYSSES S. GRANT AFTER VICTORY AT CHAMPION HILL, MISSISSIPPI, MAY 16, 1863

While the armies of Bragg and Rosencrans fought their wide-ranging campaigns in eastern Kentucky and central Tennessee, other battles were being fought further to the west, as the Union grand strategy of seizing the Mississippi River began to be put into effect. At Cairo, Illinois, the Ohio River branched off from the Mississippi and led to the Cumberland and Tennessee rivers. The control of these waterways gave Grant and Buell the maneuverability they needed. By transporting his army down the Tennessee River, Grant had struck deep into the heart of western Tennessee, effectively cutting that part of the state off from the rest of the Confederacy. His position was consolidated at Shiloh, and although the Confederate army at Corinth still remained a threat, Grant and Buell were able to dictate the pace of the campaign and determine where they

*Below: The Mississippi River, winding its way through Mississippi and Arkansas. This strategic artery was a major prize in the war. It is also home to many ghosts, from Mary Becker Greene, the riverboat pilot, to the Civil War ghosts of the river cities.*

*Above: The Union fleet anchored on the Mississippi River near Vicksburg in early 1863. The vessel in the foreground was the USS* Black Hawk, *the command ship of Admiral Porter.*

would attack next. Union gunboats on the Cumberland and Tennessee were also able to disrupt Confederate communications, as control of the two rivers effectively meant that the Confederate army was cut off from most of central Tennessee and western Kentucky.

The loss of Forts Henry and Donelson had already forced the Confederates to abandon these two regions, along with the important railroad centers of Nashville and Bowling Green. While Buell took advantage of this by strengthening his hold on these two areas and his successor Rosencrans busied himself fighting off General Bragg's Army of the Tennessee, Grant returned to the Mississippi.

It was here that the fate of the campaign in the West would be decided, and ultimately the Mississippi Campaign would seal the fate of the Confederate cause. Around the same

time that Grant's army was fighting for its life around Shiloh, Admiral David G. Farragut's Union fleet was working its way up the Mississippi Delta toward New Orleans.

On April 18, mortar schooners began bombarding the two forts that guarded the Mississippi River below New Orleans, and then on the night of April 24, his fleet steamed past the forts, initiating a dramatic fight between the forts and their supporting gunboats and the Union fleet. Although the Confederates inflicted some damage to Farragut's ships, they were unable to prevent their passage past the forts, and the following day, New Orleans fell to the Union. The forts duly surrendered, and by early May the fleet had captured Baton Rouge. With the lower part of the Mississippi River in Union hands, it was up to a newly created Union

*Opposite: In April 1862, Admiral David Glasgow Farragut (1817–1870) led his fleet past the forts defending New Orleans and so captured the city. The engagement was one of the most dramatic naval engagements of the war, and victory was achieved with relatively few casualties.*

River Flotilla to work its way down from Cairo. The plan was for the two forces to meet midway, thereby securing the river and cutting the Confederacy in two. Only a string of river forts and a small fleet of wooden gunboats lay in between the two Union forces.

In early April, the Confederate stronghold on Island No. 10 was captured, opening the way to Memphis. Followed by a whirling naval engagement fought on June 6 off Memphis, where the Union river fleet's ironclads destroyed the Confederate River Defense Fleet, the city was captured by the advancing Union river fleet and accompanying army. The Confederates had now lost control of all but the western part of Tennessee. By October, the ocean-going fleet now commanded by Flag-Officer Porter and the combined-arms force advancing down from Memphis were only a few miles apart. Only the fortified city of Vicksburg, Mississippi, prevented a linking up of the two Union fleets.

Ghost stories associated with this river campaign are few (although the river itself has a ghostly legends associated with almost every bend, from the "melodious siren" at Biloxi to the piano that plays itself at the home of the author William Faulkner at Oxford). Most of the major river cities have their share of Civil War ghosts. New Orleans is no exception. The story of the Lalaurie Mansion has already been mentioned, but during this period several other important houses experienced traumatic events that led to their associations with ghosts.

After the city fell, General Benjamin F. Butler was appointed as New Orleans's governor, and his heavy-handed approach soon earned him the hatred of the city's residents. He once hanged a man suspected of desecrating the American flag, ordered a statue of Andrew Jackson defaced, closed a newspaper that criticized him, and even decreed that any woman who insulted a member of the Union army would be treated as a common prostitute, regardless of her social standing.

"Beast Butler" certainly earned his nickname during the time he ran the city. His only positive policy was to free Louisiana's slaves, an act that at least endeared him to part of the local population.

At 1447 Constance Street, the house built by Adam Griffon in 1852 was abandoned by its owner when Butler's men took over the city, and the modest but elegant town house with its spacious, high-ceilinged rooms lay open for anyone to occupy or plunder. Butler's officers selected the property as a suitable place to house some of the Union soldiers under Butler's command, but in early May 1862, when a Union detachment commandeered the house, they made a gruesome discovery. The troops began exploring their new property, but as they climbed the stairs to the second floor, they heard the sounds of moans coming from the top floor as well as something that sounded like the rattling of chains. They opened a door into the attic and discovered the long room contained several male slaves who had been shackled to the walls of the oppressively hot room. None of the men had been fed for several days, and all

were close to dying from starvation. Two of the men had also been wounded, and in the heat the wounds had turned dangerously septic. It was a scene reminiscent of that when the secrets of the Lalaurie Mansion were revealed, but this time there seemed no indication that the slaves had been deliberately tortured or mutilated. The slaves were all taken to the city's hospital, but the reason for their makeshift prison in the attic was never explained, although it was suggested that the owner was linked to bounty hunters who tracked down runaway slaves.

The ground floor of the house became a barracks, but the upper floors were turned into a detention center, where local characters that Butler and his officers deemed suspicious could be taken and held without trial. At least one room was also used to house Union prisoners guilty of looting.

Two Union officers were caught plundering a private house in the city and were brought to the holding cells in Constance Street where they were held pending an investigation. They guards proved friendly, as after all the two officers were on the same side, and soon they shared their rations and even their whiskey with the two prisoners. It was noted that the two men were prone to singing "John Brown's Body" over and over again, a sure mark of their abolitionist fervor if nothing else. The singing was a ruse. In fact, the two men were Confederate deserters who had stolen the uniforms and wore them in an attempt to move more freely around the city, looking for plunder in abandoned homes. As they were caught

*Above left: A non-regulation Union naval officer's sword such as this would have been a cherished possession and would often be buried with its owner.*

*Left: The bombardment of Fort Donelson in February 1862 demonstrated the effectiveness of river iron-clads as well as their vulnerability. Plunging Confederate shot hit the boilers of one ironclad, filling its interior with super-heated steam. Rivermen still claim to hear the screams of the scalded men as they pass the site.*

wearing Union uniforms, they were liable to be shot as spies, so it was a risky stratagem. It became even more risky when they discovered that Butler planned to make an example of them, as a means of visibly enforcing his no-looting rule. There was going to be no escape and no reprieve for the men.

Shortly before the two men were due to be hanged, they managed to bribe the guards into lending them a pair of loaded pistols. The pair lay down on a mattress beside each other, pointed their pistols at the heart of their friend, and then they simultaneously pulled the triggers. They died instantly, the bullet to the heart sparing them a worse fate at the gallows. Their guards had been bribed to turn a blind eye, and it was not until the watch changed the following morning that the bodies were discovered, by which time

the blood was said to have been seeping through the mattress and floorboards and was dripping onto the floor of the second-floor room below.

The first mention of any ghost associated with 1447 Constance Street came in the 1920s, when the owner reported seeing strange things in his home. He refused to elaborate and then went missing, never to be found again, dead or alive. Later owners claim they heard the sound of footsteps coming from the attic, as well as the sound of moans and the rattling of chains. Locals have recounted seeing two ghostly faces peering out of the attic window overlooking the street, and some even added that they were wearing the uniforms of Union officers. Other strange happenings include the sound of singing, as if in the distance. Naturally, the song is "John Brown's Body."

*Above: The wooden ram USS* Queen of the West *attacking the Confederate ironclad CSS* Arkansas *as she lay alongside the quay at Vicksburg. The Confederate warship survived the attack, but the Union craft was captured. Engagements such as this were often short but bloody, unlike the famous, inconclusive stand-off between the ironclads USS* Monitor *and CSS* Virginia *in Hampton Roads, Virginia.*

*Right: General Pierre Gustave T. Beauregard (1818–1893) was one of the unsung heroes of the Confederacy, ordering the first shot to be fired at Fort Sumter, defeating the Union at First Manassas, and directing the defense of Charleston. After the war, he returned to New Orleans, where it is claimed his house still echoes with the sound of battle.*

During the 1930s, the house was turned into a workshop producing lamps, and in 1936 a night watchman reportedly fled the building after seeing a second-floor door open of its own accord and then hearing the sound of footsteps in the same room in which he was sitting. There was no one there, but the sound increased until he ran from the house. As he fled, he heard the sounds of drunken laughter and the abolitionist tune being sung. The workshop closed soon after. Eventually, the property was turned into a boarding house, and during the 1940s a lady tenant moved into one of the second-floor rooms. One evening she was sewing by the window when she noticed blood on her arm. She wiped it away, only to see another drop fall on her arm. Looking up, she saw blood seeping through the boards in the ceiling, then she heard the sound of that same drunken laughter and the raucous singing of the abolitionist refrain. She fled for her life.

She refused to return, and according to her relatives, as they came to collect her belongings they saw two blue-coated soldiers watching them from the attic window. The house is now in private hands, and so far the current owners have reported no strange happenings. Perhaps the two deserters finally tired of their games and left the house in peace for the first time since 1862.

Another house in the city with a ghostly Civil War link is the Beauregard-Keyes House at 1113 Chartres Street in the French Quarter. It was once the home of General Pierre Beauregard, who gave the order to fire on Fort Sumter in April 1861. Just over a year later, his house fell into Union hands. The general played a major part in winning a stunning victory at First Manassas and then commanded part of the Confederate army at Shiloh. He spent much of the remainder of the war defending the port of Charleston, keeping the blockading Union fleet at bay. After the war, he returned to his home in New Orleans, and his house was returned to him by its Union occupiers. He refused offers of command in both the Egyptian and Romanian armies, and instead he became a chief engineer of a railroad company, working on restoring rail links across the war-ravaged South. He also became a partner in a street-car company in his home city.

His reputation was somewhat tarnished by his association with the Louisiana Lottery, where as a supervisor he was accused of deliberately drawing the tickets of his cronies. This scandal blew over, and after serving as Louisiana's adjutant general, he retired to write histories of the war, including his lucid *Battle of Manassas.* The old general finally died in 1893.

There were no accounts that his house was haunted during his lifetime, but in 1909 it was sold to a Mr. Giacona, who, it seems, had Mafia connections. During a bungled attempt to kidnap him and his family, three gunmen were killed in a shoot-out in the house. By 1925, the Giacona family planned to turn the property into a pasta factory, but concerned residents banded together to purchase the property for the city, a lasting tribute to the Confederate general who lived there. The

*Right As suggested earlier, could it simply be the age and the grandeur of southern mansions like this one outside the city of New Orleans (now on Chalmette Battlefield National Park) that persuades people of the existence of supernatural phenomena within their walls? Not entirely: the reports of ghostly sightings at the equally impressive Shirley plantation in Charles City, Virginia, (below) are numerous. But the 1815 edifice above? Nothing.*

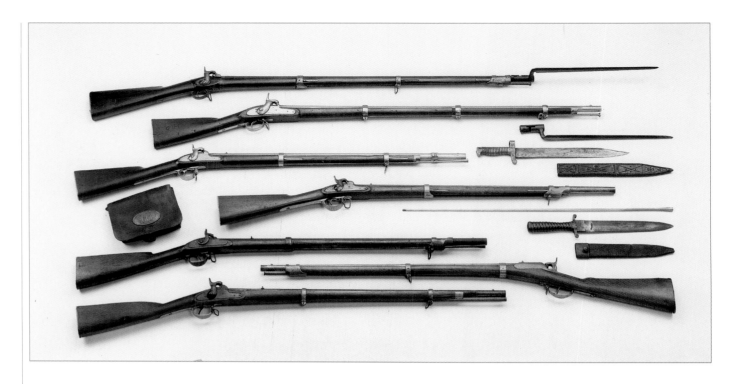

building is now a National Historic Site and is open to the public. It was in the early 1950s that people working in the house or passing by in the street reported hearing the sounds of battle coming from within the building itself, although the exact source of the sound seems to have moved and so defied any attempt to track down its source. It was almost as if the whole house had become a battleground, and a Civil War one at that. The guns being fired were not modern automatic weapons or even the gangster-related weapons used by the Giacona family. The sounds were those of muzzle-loading muskets, cannon, horses, and bayonet charges, as if Shiloh or First Manassas were being fought all over again for the benefit of the general-turned-historian who wrote his military memoirs there. Today, the tour guides say that these stories were either made up or else the sounds have not been heard for many decades. It does seem that ghostly sightings or sounds last for a period until something happens that brings them to an end, whether the discovery of a corpse, or more likely, the lapse of public interest in such seemingly tall tales. While many ghost hunters

would be delighted to hear the sounds of battle again, it is probably better that if anything supernatural was causing these sounds, it seems to have been pacified.

Further up the river, the great plantation houses half-hidden behind the levees guarding them from the Mississippi River all have their fair share of ghosts, but most of these stories lie outside the scope of this book. Some have direct ghostly associations with the war, such as Longwood, outside Natchez, Mississippi. As an example of what owners of these plantation homes experienced, it is worth providing a summary of Longwood's story. The house was still under construction when the war began. The half-finished mansion was occupied by Union troops as they advanced up the river from New Orleans. The owner, Dr. Haller Nutt, and his family were forced to live in the cellar of their dream home. The cotton plantations that surrounded it were looted, and the Nutt family were never able to finish the building. Today, it is run by a local gardening society, who claim that the ghosts of Dr. Nutt and his wife still appear in the house and

*Above: A selection of Confederate muskets, ranging from the primitive smoothbore weapon at the top to more sophisticated rifled muskets and carbines below, along with their associated bayonets. It was claimed that it took more than one hundred pounds of lead shot to kill a soldier, as even the most modern rifled musket was notoriously inaccurate.*

*Opposite: These personal effects of Confederate artillerymen show how a typical Southern gunner was attired. Artifacts such as these bring the past alive, a haunting reminder of the men who fought and died in the most deadly war on American soil.*

*Above: The ghosts of Union gunners are still supposed to be heard firing their artillery pieces on several battlefields, including Shiloh, Murfreesboro, and Bentonville.*

grounds, keeping a wary eye on the visitors who come to see the site's attractions.

The Mississippi River cuts through the "cradle of the Civil War" from Memphis down to New Orleans, but despite its strategic importance, only one major battle was fought for its control after the loss of New Orleans and Memphis. The city of Vicksburg dominated the Mississippi in 1863, and the battle fought for its control was the most decisive of the entire war in the Western theater. It is hardly surprising that the city also has a substantial number of Civil War ghost stories associated with it.

# Ghosts of Vicksburg

*"In the trenches around Vicksburg . . . the men in the outer lines would call to each other to stop firing for a while, they 'wanted to get out into fresh air!' The call was always heeded."*

GENERAL GORDON'S REMINISCENCES, 1903

Vicksburg was once described as the "Gibraltar of the West," a reference to the British-held rocky fortress that dominated the entrance into the Mediterranean Sea. In October 1862, General Grant became the commander of the "Department of the Mississippi," the overall Union commander during the coming campaign. In December, he ordered his subordinate General Sherman to attempt an attack on the city from the north, but this was rebuffed at Chickasaw

Bluffs. Grant adopted a bold plan of attack, first capturing the Confederate Fort Hindman, which prevented any flanking attack from Arkansas, then moving the bulk of his army downriver to within a few miles of Vicksburg itself. On April 30, he launched his risky masterstroke, landing his army of more than 40,000 men thirty miles downriver from the city at Bruinsburg. He had abandoned his lines of communication, and from that point on, his army was on its own.

*Opposite: Although the Union guns ringing in Vicksburg have been silent for almost 150 years, the effects of the siege were remembered long after the city surrendered on July 4, 1863. The inhabitants of Vicksburg only celebrated July 4 again after World War II. Meanwhile, other reminders of the conflict can be found in many of the city's old mansions.*

*Left: The once bustling river port of Vicksburg, Mississippi, was subjected to a grueling siege in the summer of 1863, and the ghosts of that harrowing period are still said to stalk the streets and waterfront of the city.*

Only victory could save it from disaster. He marched east, capturing the state capital of Jackson on May 14, then turning west toward Vicksburg itself. General Pemberton's defenders were taken by surprise, and after a token resistance at Champion's Hill and the Big Black River, they fell back inside the defenses of Vicksburg. Grant laid siege to the city, and by the end of it soldiers and civilians alike were starving inside of it. More than two hundred artillery pieces pounded the city day and night, forcing the residents to abandon their homes and take refuge in caves in the cliffs lining the river. People fought over dead dogs in the street, and in the end, the soldiers were reduced to eating rats and boiling horse harnesses to make soup. Disease ravaged the defending ranks, and the remains of elegant houses were virtually destroyed by artillery, while any wood or furnishings that survived were used to keep the population and the garrison warm at night. It was a grueling seven weeks, but the outcome was never in doubt.

On July 4, 1863, the day after Pickett's Charge in Gettysburg, the Confederates surrendered Vicksburg to Grant's Union army. 30,000 ragged and half-starved Confederate soldiers were led away into captivity, a loss in manpower that the South could not afford. Although a few minor garrisons remained on its banks, for all effective purposes, the entire Mississippi River was now in Union hands. With the Confederacy split into two, Vicksburg gone, and Lee in retreat, the tide had turned, and whatever lay ahead, an ultimate Union victory seemed inevitable. Grant sent

a telegram to President Lincoln, offering him Vicksburg as a Fourth of July present. The date itself wouldn't be celebrated in Vicksburg until after the end of World War II.

The city that had endured forty-eight days of siege, of shelling, and of starvation seemed to have suffered almost as much as the troops and civilians who sheltered inside it. As the war moved away from Vicksburg and the city became a Union base, life returned to some semblance of normality, and today it bears relatively few scars from those bleak days in the summer of 1863. However, there are enough ghost stories in circulation to suggest that for some souls the torment of the siege and its aftermath still continues.

Probably the best known ghost story to survive from this period concerns the McRaven House, a stately building commandeered by the Union authorities soon after the city was captured, and where the local garrison commander Colonel Wilson established his military headquarters. Attached to his staff was a Mississippi-born abolitionist named McPherson who had spent several years living in the city before the war. He decided to offer his services to the Union, and when Grant captured the city in July 1863, Captain McPherson was attached to Colonel Wilson's staff. This meant that he was quartered in the McRaven House, where he acted as a liaison officer, maintaining links between the city's inhabitants and its military occupier. He was widely regarded as a traitor to the city and the state, and given the level of feeling in Vicksburg at the time, it seems less than sur-

*Above: An encampment of troops from Logan's division of the Union Army of the Tennessee encamped in front of Vicksburg shortly after the city surrendered. Strangely, most of the city's ghost stories are associated with the aftermath of the siege rather than with the fighting itself.*

prising that one evening McPherson failed to return to his quarters. Over the next few days, Colonel Wilson and his garrison searched the city for the young officer, but no trace of him was ever found. That was when he reappeared as a ghostly vision.

About ten days after the disappearance, Colonel Wilson retired to his chambers and went to bed, but he was woken in the middle of the night by the sound of movement in his room. He rose and searched the bedroom but found nothing to explain the noises. Rather than return to bed, he sat in an armchair close to the fireplace, facing the door to his bedroom. If anyone was sneaking into his

chambers, he planned to catch them in the act. Then after several minutes, he felt the temperature drop and a strong cold wind blow in his face. By this time, the Colonel was somewhat alarmed, but he was still unprepared for the materialization in front of him: the image of Captain McPherson. The ghost appeared to be dripping with water, his face was badly battered, and blood covered much of his upper body. The apparition spoke to the Colonel, explained that he had been murdered, and even named the culprit. McPherson's ghost then continued, suggesting that the Colonel call off the search, since his body would never be discovered. He then

recommended that instead of bringing his killer to justice, the Colonel should let the matter rest, in order to encourage a spirit of reconciliation in the city. The ghost then disappeared.

True to his word, the Colonel dropped the investigation, but from then on he kept a watchful eye on certain prominent members of the city's residents. According to the legend, the ghost of the Captain continues to return to the house from time to time, repeating the details of his murder and delivering the same message of reconciliation. Visitors to the house have also seen the ghosts of Civil War soldiers walking in the corridors, and even a woman with long auburn hair pacing the floor of a bedroom. It has been claimed that other ghosts have

also been seen in the house, including that of the wartime owner John Bobb, who was shot by drunken Union soldiers after he tried to drive them off his property by throwing bricks at them. While these tales are not that unusual, the sheer number of ghost sightings have led the McRaven House to be dubbed "the most haunted house in Mississippi." The grisly nature of Captain McPherson's death and the appeasing approach of his supposed ghost both seem somewhat unusual, and thus stand out among other wartime ghost stories.

On Vicksburg's East First Street, the Anchuca mansion built by Richard Archer in 1837 is said to be haunted by his willful daughter, who so closely resembled her father she was nicknamed "Archie."

*Above: Cedar Grove mansion at Vicksburg was built in 1840 and remains a sparkling reminder of the glamour of the antebellum plantation lifestyle, despite being shelled by Union gunboats during the siege. It is also said to be haunted by the ghosts of its pro-Federal owner and his family.*

*Above: A small engagement was fought at Poison Spring, Arkansas, in April 1864, and it is claimed that the ghost of a wounded black soldier in the uniform of a Union infantryman still haunts the woods around the site. Reputedly, he was one of the black prisoners executed by Confederate troops after the battle.*

The young lady supposedly died of a broken heart when her father refused to let her marry her impoverished sweetheart, and today her ghost is still said to haunt the house, the figure wearing a brown dress and standing beside a fireplace in the parlor. At the time of the Civil War, the house was owned by Joseph Davis, the brother of the Confederate president.

The Duff Green mansion on the same street was used as a hospital during the Siege of Vicksburg, and owners of the property have reported hearing the sounds of scuffled footsteps on the second floor of the house, but on investigation it was found that the floor was deserted.

Could these have been the ghosts of Confederate soldiers being brought to the operating table, or even, as has been suggested, the souls of the dead soldiers searching for the limbs that the surgeon amputated there? The property is now run as a guest house, so visitors can listen out for the ghosts during their stay.

Finally, the second-most haunted house in Vicksburg is probably Cedar Grove, built in 1840 and one of the largest and most elegant mansions in the area. During the war, it was owned by John Klein, a staunch opponent of secession and a loyal Union man. He was supported in his unpopular political stance by his Ohio-born wife, who was said to be a relative of Grant's gifted General Sherman. Klein's pro-Union stance led to him being ostracized by Vicksburg society and may have been a factor in the shooting of his teenage son William during the period of Union occupation following the city's fall. It is said that John Klein's ghost still appears in the parlor, his appearance always linked with the smell of a smoking pipe. Sounds of footsteps and even screams have been heard on the stairs, where the ghost of Mrs. Klein has been seen from time to time. Throughout the house, the sound of children playing can sometimes be heard; the Kleins had ten children, one of whom was shot and three who died while still very young. To complete the picture, the mansion's ballroom is also said to be haunted by a young antebellum ghost, the spirit of a lady who was supposed to have committed suicide in that room.

There is a substantial collection of supernatural associations with the Confederacy's fortress city on the Mississippi, and the sheer number of accounts of haunting and strange occurrences in the city is enough to make Vicksburg one of the most haunted cities in the South.

# Chickamauga and Chattanooga

*"I think we may retrieve the disaster of this morning . . . The rebel ammunition must be nearly exhausted. Ours fast failing. If we can hold out an hour more it will be all right."*

GENERAL GARFIELD TO GENERAL ROSENCRANS, SEPTEMBER 20, 1863

While the Siege of Vicksburg was reaching its climax, General Rosencrans finally set his Army of the Cumberland into motion, and a series of outflanking moves were enough to force General Bragg's Confederate Army of the Tennessee back to its base in Chattanooga. By August, Bragg had abandoned the city and had fallen even farther back to the south, into Georgia. However, he had a plan. Reinforcements had joined him from eastern Tennessee and Virginia, meaning he now had 60,000 men under his command, roughly the same number that Rosencrans had at his disposal. The Union army continued its pursuit of Bragg, and by mid-September, it was advancing on

*Below: The great bend in the Tennessee River with Chattanooga in the distance, viewed from the summit of Lookout Mountain, the setting for the "Battle in the Clouds."*

128

a broad front into Georgia and northeastern Alabama. His plan was to cut off Bragg's line of retreat to the south, thereby forcing him to give battle. Rosencrans certainly achieved his wish, but it was his army that would be on the defensive, not Bragg's.

One of Rosencrans's advancing columns of 14,000 men, commanded by General Crittenden, had reached the banks of the Chickamauga Creek at Lee & Gordon's Mills, some twelve miles south of Chattanooga. Bragg decided to fall upon this isolated army corps before Rosencrans could reinforce it with his remaining columns.

However, Bragg delayed his attack until his troops were in place, and during this five-day hiatus, Rosencrans joined Crittenden with the corps of Generals Thomas and McCook. Bragg, still insistent on launching his attack, hoped that surprise and the heavily wooded terrain would work in his favor. If the Confederates managed to sever the Union army's line of communications back to Chattanooga, then the Army of the Cumberland would be in grave danger.

The attack began on the morning of September 19, when General Forrest's cavalry, moving to cut the Lafayette Road to the

*Left: Major General Thomas L .Crittenden (1819–1893) commanded a Union corps at Chicka-mauga, and by the end of the battle, almost one in three of his men were killed or seriously wounded.*

*Above: The climax of the battle took place on September 20 near Snodgrass Hill, where Major General Thomas's corps was assailed on three sides by Confederates. The site is now reported to be haunted by a terrible, vengeful specter called "Old Green Eyes."*

north of the Union army, ran into columns of General Thomas's corps marching south along the road towards Lee & Gordon's Mill. Both sides fed in reinforcements to the fighting, which then developed into a full-scale battle. Thomas's corps bore the brunt of the Confederate attacks, but despite being pushed back a mile though the woods, the Union line remained intact, denying Bragg the breakthrough he needed to encircle Rosencrans's army. The fighting began again the following morning (September 20), with Bragg launching General Polk into the fray with his entire corps on the right, while Lee's principal lieutenant, General Longstreet,

attacked on the left. The latter was responsible for the first success of the day. Finding a gap in the Union line north of Lee & Gordon's Mills, he poured the bulk of his command into the gap, splitting the Union line and allowing him to attack McCook's corps in the flank.

The Union right wing collapsed, and by early afternoon, two Union corps were fleeing in disorder toward Chattanooga. Only Thomas's corps remained in the field, but his men held firm, earning their commander the accolade, the "Rock of Chickamauga." He held on until nightfall, then pulled back toward Chattanooga, leaving the field to the

victorious Confederates. Although Bragg had won a spectacular victory, the cost had been high; an estimated 18,454 Confederates and 16,170 Union soldiers were killed or seriously wounded during the bitter two-day fight in the woods of Chickamauga, 34,624 men in total, or a third of the participants. For the Confederates it was a blood-soaked victory they could ill afford.

For the next two months, the Union Army of the Cumberland in Chattanooga licked its wounds, while Bragg's army occupied the hills overlooking the town from the south. Chattanooga was, in effect, a city under siege. The situation changed in late October, when General Grant arrived to take charge. A plan was drawn up for an assault on the Confederate positions, and as Union reinforcements arrived, Grant prepared his men for the coming battle. The return of Longstreet's corps to the east meant that Bragg now had just 40,000 men, almost half the number of troops available to Grant. The battle began on November 23, when the Union army marched out of the city and deployed in the open ground between the Tennessee River and the Confederate positions on Missionary Ridge.

The next day, General Hooker attacked the Confederates on Lookout Mountain, and against all expectations, his men drove the defenders from the summit. The steepness of Lookout Mountain meant that the Confederates were unable to depress their artillery far enough to cover the lower slopes, giving Hooker's men the chance to approach their positions without suffering heavy casualties

*Left: Union troops on the summit of Lookout Mountain after their victory there on November 24, 1863. Today, the summit is said to be haunted, not by Civil War soldiers, but by the ghosts of those who committed suicide by throwing themselves from the rocks.*

during the climb. This "Battle in the Clouds," as it was dubbed, was the turning point. With the Confederate line turned, Bragg should have retreated, but for once he decided to remain and fight. On November 25, General Thomas's men charged up Missionary Ridge, supported by a flanking attack against the Confederate right launched by General Sherman. Again, the assault succeeded in throwing the defenders from the top of the ridge, and with Sherman on his flank, Bragg had no option but to order a general retreat. Both sides lost around 6,000 men killed or wounded in the battles for Chattanooga, but Grant was the clear victor. With Chattanooga safely in Union hands, he was free to launch his troops south into Georgia. From that point

forward, there was no stopping the Union army on the western front.

The two battles fought in dense woods or mountaintops had been costly, and it took weeks to recover the bodies from the two battlefields. Even then, bodies remained behind, lost in the thickets of Chickamauga or hidden in the rocks of Lookout Mountain or Missionary Ridge. It is little wonder that ghost stories and tales of strange supernatural happenings began to appear, making Chickamauga one of the most haunted battlefields of the western theater.

The very name Chickamauga was enough to make some people shiver with dread. For centuries before the two great Civil War armies fought each other beside the Chickamauga Creek, the area had been

*Above: During the fighting near the Lafayette Road, the musket and artillery fire was so intense that the trees were stripped of their leaves and branches, giving the battlefield a surreal and menacing appearance, even after the bodies were laid to rest.*

regarded as sacred and haunted. In Native American folklore, a great battle was supposed to have been fought at Chickamauga between the Cherokees on one side and some unnamed tribal alliance on the other.

The name of the creek, "Chickamauga," means "River of Death" in Cherokee, and in September 1863, the small river lived up to its name. Today, much of the battlefield forms part of a National Battlefield Park run by the National Park Service, giving visitors the chance to imagine what it must have been like during those long hours of fighting. The battlefield is a melancholy spot; on my last visit, the weather was clear on a crisp winter's afternoon, but by mid-afternoon a thick mist descended, making it difficult to drive or even to read interpretative panels. It was an unforgettable feeling, standing shrouded by mist on a spot where thousands had died. Others have reported the same meteorological phenomena, and although experts have provided rational explanations for it, the experience is still a disturbing one.

Others have provided a less scientific explanation. Locals say that if you drive into Battlefield Park at night, the fog will not be seen before entering or after leaving it. It only happens on the battlefield itself. While it is probably a phenomenon associated with the water of the Chickamauga Creek, there are those who say the smoke represents the lingering effects of the gunfire that crashed through those same woods almost 150 years ago. A few even claim it isn't mist at all but a conglomeration of the spirits of the dead. While this is almost certainly just fantasy, the existence of the mist or fog is a verifiable fact.

The battlefield also developed a more verifiable but still chilling reputation as the perfect spot to dump bodies, the victims of shootings in Atlanta or Chattanooga. Increased nighttime patrolling has largely put a stop to the tradition, but it remains just another grisly twist in the history of the River of Death. It seems that some of the young men who died close to its banks in 1863 have refused to lie in peace.

*Left: The opening shots of the Battle of Chicka-mauga, as Confederate artillerymen open fire on Union cavalry near Reeds Bridge, September 18, 1863. The bridge was named after a local farmer-turned-soldier whose wife is still said to haunt the battlefield.*

The most persistent ghost story associated with the Chickamauga battlefield is that of the "White Lady." After the fighting ended at nightfall on September 20, the area around Lafayette Road was covered with bodies, guns, and the detritus of battle. While General Thomas withdrew his remaining troops to the northwest, soldiers and local civilians alike began the task of seeking out those who were still alive. The wounded were taken to makeshift casualty stations and hospitals, then the work of recovering the bodies of the fallen began. While some were transported to their home towns for burial, others were interred close to the spot where they had died. It would have been an agonizing process for friends or relatives, scanning the bodies of horribly mutilated men in the hope that a missing soldier's corpse could be found and brought away for burial.

The Union dead suffered an even worse fate, as many remained where they had fallen for two months, and some were only laid to rest when Sherman's army passed through the battlefield in the weeks following Grant's victory at Chattanooga. Many were simply buried where they lay, or thrown into long,

striplike pits. Others from both sides were buried in unmarked graves, some of which could contain several bodies. Since the locations of these burials were never properly recorded, the Park Service employees will still occasionally find burial sites hidden deep in the woods. Others will probably never be found.

One of the southern civilians who combed the battlefield after the fighting ended was Abigail Reed, the fiancée or newlywed bride of a Confederate soldier who was posted as missing. She asked everyone she met, but nobody knew where her fiancé's body lay. What was striking about her was that she wore a white dress, presumably the one she wore or had planned to wear on her wedding day. His body was never found, but Abigail Reed never gave up her search. She became a common sight on the battlefields, combing the ground until dark, when she lit a lantern and kept going. She always wore the same white dress. According to the story, she died a few years later, stricken down by grief, and appropriately, she was buried in her white dress. Locals claim that the light of her lantern can still be seen at night, flickering

*Opposite: Even today, the battlefield of Chicka-mauga is a particularly eerie place and is frequently blanketed in a thick, disorienting mist. While good meteorological explanations have been offered, there are those who suggest the mist is a supernatural phenomenon.*

through the trees as she still searches for her lover. Appropriately enough, the light always seems to move in a purposeful way, rather than at random like the accounts of other ghostly lights on Civil War battlefields. She can also be seen in daylight, picking her way through the mist-shrouded trees as she combs the ground. In recent years, park rangers reported that visitors to the battlefield who seemed to know nothing of the story described seeing a lady dressed in a white period costume, who seemed real enough until they approached. Then they noticed a slight glow to her pale skin, and despite their exclamations, she continued with her search as if the people never existed. Today, Reed's Bridge over Chickamauga Creek on the eastern edge of the battlefields is said to have been named after the lady and her family, who lived in the area.

The tales of strange happenings in Battlefield Park are not limited to sightings of the "White Lady of Chickamauga." Both park rangers and visitors have reported hearing the sounds of men shouting and fighting, or even of horses passing them at speed, as if a ghostly, horse-drawn artillery battery is still cantering to where it is needed most. Other witnesses claim they have heard the sounds of wounded and dying men crying out for help and for water, while a few profess to have seen whole columns of ghostly soldiers marching along the roads through the woods. There is one account that a headless horseman has been seen riding through the woods of Chickamauga. This echoes a battlefield account from a Confederate soldier

fighting on the last day of the battle near Lafayette Road who recalled seeing an officer's head taken off by a round shot, but the horse and rider kept on riding.

Perhaps the most persistent of these ghost tales is that of "Old Green Eyes." Rangers and visitors who have been in the park during the hours of darkness have reported seeing what look like a pair of glowing green eyes coming toward them. The image is often associated with the sound of wailing or moaning, as if from a wounded soldier. The same pair of eyes have also been seen by those driving by, or at least that is what they claimed after running their cars off the road into the trees. The insurance claims would have made particularly interesting reading.

Old Green Eyes has been identified with an old Native American tale of a monster who inhabited the banks of the Chickamauga, part human but mostly wild animal. According to the legend, the creature has glowing green eyes, long, fair-colored hair, and a hideously misshapen jaw nearly covered by a pair of fangs. It has also been claimed that this creature was seen roaming the battlefield after the final day of fighting on Snodgrass Hill, where Thomas's men made their stand. Another attempt to identify Old Green Eyes claims that he was a Confederate soldier who was blown to pieces by close-range canister fire during the battle. All that was left of the soldier was his head, as the rest of his body was splattered through the trees and was deemed unrecoverable. Today, the head still haunts the battlefield, its glowing green eyes searching for the rest of its long-lost body.

*Above: Snodgrass Hill on the Chickamauga battle-field, the site of Thomas's stand on the second day. This clearing was carpeted with bodies by the time the fighting drew to a close and must have resembled a scene from hell.*

Ghost-story writer Richard Winer reported a conversation with Edward Tinney, a park ranger who encountered Old Green Eyes in 1981. He was conducting a night-time patrol of the park when he felt a sudden and inexplicable drop in temperature. Then he saw Old Green Eyes approaching him out of the darkness. Fortunately, the "thing" kept on walking:

When it passed me I could see his hair was long like a woman's. The eyes—I'll never forget those eyes—they were glaring, almost greenish-orange in color, flashing like some sort of wild animal. The teeth were long and pointed like fangs. It was wearing a dark cape that seemed to be flapping in the wind, but there was no wind. I didn't know whether to run or scream or what. Then the headlights of an approaching car came blazing through the fog, and the thing disappeared right in front of me.

Tinney said that he was very far from super-stitious before the encounter and viewed sto-ries about ghosts in Battlefield Park with a large degree of skepticism. Now he is con-vinced something is out there:

You know he's watching. We all know he's watching us. It's enough to make the hair stand up on the back of your neck . . . and I'm not a superstitious man.

Whether such stories are believable or not, the battlefield is certainly a hauntingly mov-ing place, where it would be all too easy to imagine the dark deeds of history or the even stranger goings on of the supernatural. When the battlefield is shrouded in its own mist or covered by darkness, it makes some kind of sense to think that if ever ghosts still prowled a Civil War battlefield, this would be the place to encounter them.

# The Last Specters of Battle

*"Heap with kind hands her costly funeral pyre,*
*And thus, with paean sung and anthem rolled,*
*Give her unspotted to the God of Fire."*

ON CHARLESTON'S FALL, FROM THE FOE AT THE GATES, DR. J. D. BRUNS

After his victory at Chattanooga, General Grant was called to Washington, where he was given command of the whole Union army. Command of the western armies was given to Grant's trusted subordinate, General Sherman. In May 1864, Sherman led his 100,000 men south into Georgia, and although Bragg had been replaced by the far more able General Joseph E. Johnston, the Confederates were outnumbered almost two to one. Although they managed to delay Sherman, they couldn't stop him. By late July, he lay outside Atlanta, and a bitter series of battles were fought in defense of the city before Sherman succeeded in outflanking the city's defenses. By this time, Johnston had been replaced by the fire-eating Texan, General Hood, but even he proved powerless

*Below: Savannah fell to General Sherman on December 20. The general wired President Lincoln that he presented the city to him as a Christmas gift. A shabby present, since Union troops burned most of the city to the ground.*

140

*Above: General William T. Sherman (1820–1891) cut a destructive swathe from Atlanta to the coast, a campaign that became a byword for wanton destruction and lived up to Sherman's own maxim that "War is Hell."*

in the face of Sherman's juggernaut. On September 1, the Confederates abandoned Atlanta, and it looked as if Georgia lay wide open to the Union army.

Hood was never one to patiently wait for his opponent, but his diversionary plan was bold even for him. During September and October, he bypassed Sherman's troops and headed west and north, crossing into Alabama and then back into Tennessee. He then led his Army of the Tennessee towards Nashville, bypassing a Union garrison at Columbia to fall on another force at Franklin. Although Hood won the battle, his losses had been heavy—over 6,000 men. By early December, the Confederates had reached Nashville, but the icy weather prevented any fighting and bought the Union defenders time to call in reinforcements. On December 15, General Thomas had 54,000 men in Nashville facing Hood's 24,000. The Union army attacked, and by the end of the day, the survivors of Hood's army were in full retreat.

While this was taking place, Sherman launched his own offensive. Later known to history as "Sherman's March to the Sea," the campaign began on November 15, when 68,000 veteran Union troops poured out of Atlanta and headed southeast toward Savannah, cutting a forty-mile-wide swathe through the countryside and pulling up railroad tracks, burning plantations, and destroying crops. The Confederates had no army left to stop him, and Savannah fell on December 20. Sherman then continued north into South Carolina, driving the Confederates before him. Charleston fell on February 18, and by early March, Sherman was in North Carolina. The remnants of the Confederate garrisons on the Atlantic seaboard were gathered into one last army, and when these were joined by the survivors of Hood's army, the force commander, General Joseph E. Johnston, was ready to stand and fight.

The result was the last full-scale engagement of the war. His 20,000 men were gathered around the North Carolina town of Bentonville, and it was there that they made their stand. In fact, it was Johnston who attacked first, when on March 19, he led an assault on Sherman's leading column. Despite being pushed back, a Union rally restored the position and averted disaster.

Two days later, it was Sherman's turn to attack, sending troops around the Confederate rear while he pinned them to his front. The fighting resumed on March 21, but the result was inconclusive. Outnumbered and outgunned, Johnston withdrew his army under cover of darkness. Just over a month later, he surrendered his force, the last Confederate army in the field, so marking the end of a war that had lasted for four blood-soaked years and cost the lives of over

*Above: General John B. Hood (1831–1879) assumed command of the Confederate Army of the Tennessee in July 1864. Having lost Atlanta, he led the army west and north back into Tennessee, where it was destroyed in the two bloody battles of Franklin and Nashville.*

*Above: Supply wagons, sutler's carts, and camp followers bringing up the rear of Sherman's army during the "March to the Sea." Like the troops before them, these people preyed on the Georgians they passed as if trying to inflict retribution for the war on the state's civilian population.*

half a million men. The traumatic effects of Sherman's March to the Sea remained long after the fighting ended. The scars of burned plantation homes and farms served as a vivid reminder of the horrors of total war. Though numerous ghosts have been associated with buildings or places in Atlanta, Nashville, or Savannah, few related directly to the fighting during this last phase of the war or with the march to the sea. However, both the battlefields of Franklin, Tennessee, and Bentonville, North Carolina, had long been associated with the ghosts of men who fought and died in these last terrible battles.

One of the most inspiring commanders in the Confederate Army of the Tennessee was General Patrick Cleburne, whose ability as a fighting commander was amply demonstrated at Murfreesboro, Chickamauga, Chattanooga, and Atlanta. The Southern press went so far as to call him the "Stonewall of the West." When General Hood assumed command of the battered little army and led it north into Tennessee, Cleburne and his men marched with him. When Hood's army reached Franklin, they discovered the city was occupied by General Schofield's large corps of 30,000 men. Although the Union line was well entrenched and the approaches covered by artillery, Hood decided to attack. Cleburne and his men were selected to lead the assault. Later, the open ground in front of Schofield's defenses was dubbed the "Valley of Death," but Cleburne willingly led the

near-suicidal frontal attack, hoping to gain a foothold in the Union defensive line that Hood could exploit with the rest of the army. The last words he spoke before the assault were to a fellow officer: "Well Govan, if we are to die, let us die as men." In late afternoon, Cleburne launched his attack with 10,000 men. Another 10,000 followed behind, ready to pour through any breach. Cleburne had two horses shot under him, but he continued to lead the attack on foot,

waving his cap in the air to encourage his men. Somehow the attackers reached the enemy line, and fierce hand-to-hand fighting raged for over five hours before the Union defenders gave up the fight. As darkness covered the battlefield, Schofield withdrew his army to Nashville, leaving 2,300 men behind. The Confederate casualties were far greater, Hood's army losing more that 6,000 men that day. One of those killed was Cleburne, shot within yards of the Union line. His body

*Above:* Lines of Confederate prisoners await transportation north to prisoner-of-war camps. During the fall of 1864, the Confederate armies in the western theater simply melted away, with many troops surrendering while others deserted and made their way home.

*Above right: The ruins of Charleston, South Carolina, after the city fell to the Union in February 1865. The few buildings that remained undamaged after years of bombardment were destroyed by vengeful Union troops, leaving the city a wasted shell.*

was taken to the nearby Carnton House, where he was buried, but after the war his remains were exhumed and moved to Helena, Arkansas, where the general was finally laid to rest. Many of his men were buried in the grounds of Carnton House, which is now a Confederate cemetery. It is also haunted. Footsteps have been heard pacing the empty second-floor balcony of the house, and the local legend is that this restless ghost belongs to Patrick Cleburne.

The general's ghost has not only been heard but also seen; in 1986, a security guard encountered the figure of a man, dressed in the uniform of a Confederate general, looking down at him from the balcony. When challenged, the figure disappeared into thin air. Two years later, the figure was seen again, this time sitting on the porch. As the figure appeared in the headlights of a car, it rose, turned away, then disappeared. Once again he was wearing a long gray coat, but his face remained in shadow. The door leading to the balcony has also been locked if the key were left in it, even though the staff members swear the door was unlocked when they last saw it.

Other visitors to the property have occasionally reported seeing the men Cleburne led into battle. As in so many other cases, at first they thought the figures dressed in Confederate uniforms were reenactors, paid to walk around the property and the graves. When they inquired at the house, they were told that no such reenactors were on the property. While the identity of the ghost that supposedly haunts the balcony of the Carnton House has never been identified, staff and locals refer to him as "the general" and are certain that the spirit of General Cleburne still paces the balcony, brooding over the loss of so many of his men that late afternoon and evening in November 1864.

Bentonville has its own ghostly tale. When the fighting ended, some 3,000 Confederates became casualties, while over 1,600 Union troops were killed or wounded in the three-day fight. The little town of Bentonville lay in ruins, but many of its ruined buildings were turned into hospitals and mortuaries. As General Johnston continued his retreat into North Carolina, Sherman's army moved off in pursuit, leaving just a handful of medical staff and burial parties behind to clean up the battlefield, tend the wounded, and bury the dead. A farm close to the battlefield belonged to a John Harper and his family, and when the Union army marched, about sixty grievously wounded soldiers were left

behind in their farmhouse and its surrounding buildings, tended to by a small medical staff. Many of these men had no chance of survival and succumbed to their wounds in the weeks that followed. The dead were buried on the farm, but according to ghost-

*Below: The burning of Columbia, South Carolina's state capital. Thousands of inhabitants were forced to flee for their lives.*

*Right: General Sherman's army enters Savannah, Georgia, unopposed and apparently in good order, in December 1864, five weeks from Atlanta.*

story writer Keith Toney, their spirits still remain at large. Occupants have heard the sound of wounded men moaning in pain or the sound of voices when they know they were alone in the house. Local hunters claim to have witnessed a ghostly fight between two bodies of Civil War soldiers while walking in the woods near the farm. The Harper family themselves seem to haunt the farmhouse, along with the wounded men in their care.

In 1990, one family of tourists saw a "living history" display of the house as it would have looked in 1865, with wounded soldiers lying in rows behind the house, while Mr. Harper moved around them. They were later told that no such reenactment event had ever been staged at the property. What exactly had they seen? In other parts of the battlefield, the sounds of fighting, of gunfire, and of men shouting have been heard from time to time, while others report seeing lights flickering over the battlefield at night.

An even more unusual report is from a group of visitors who imagined they saw the battle being fought out in the clouds over the battlefield itself, an account that ties in with local claims that on certain moonlit nights, the sounds of battle can be heard and the flash of weapons and gunfire seen in the air, although they add that this only happens around the time of the anniversary of the fighting. Whether there is any truth in these legends or not, the ghost tales associated with the Bentonville battlefield are quite unique, unlike many others encountered on other Civil War fields of battle, which tend

to include the same themes. Is there something behind these unique accounts, or are the tales just the inventions of those who, for their own reasons, want to put Bentonville on the ghost-hunting map? The battlefield is atmospheric enough with or without any ghosts. As the site of the Confederacy's last stand, Bentonville seems to sum up the futility of this final stage of the War Between the States, where so many men died to defend a lost cause or else died to forcibly reestablish unity to a divided and embittered nation.

*Right: The remains of a damaged coastal-defense gun carriage on the Charleston waterfront stands sentinel over the war-ravaged town. Although Charleston is supposed to have numerous resident ghosts, surprisingly few of them date from the Civil War.*

# GHOSTS OF HOME

NOT ALL THE GHOSTS ASSOCIATED with the Civil War are found on the battlefield or even the houses turned into temporary hospitals or morgues on the edges of these fields of battle. The long and bloody war also had a profound effect on those far from the fighting; the wives or families of the soldiers; the farmers and artisans who produced food, weapons, and clothing for the troops; the men incarcerated in the hellholes of prisons in both the North and the South; and even the leaders and politicians who directed the course of the war. For them, the harsh reality of the war was often just as vivid as it was for the troops on the battlefield. The following selection of accounts reflects this, from the ghosts of starving prisoners of war in the terrible prison camps to the spirits of the great and the good whose political actions divided the nation in the first place.

*Left: The monument in the cemetery in Andersonville, Georgia, watches over the graves of the Union soldiers who perished in the camp. The cemetery itself is supposed to be haunted, as are several other locations around the site.*

# The Ghostly Lincoln Legacy

*"Sorrow comes to all . . . Perfect relief is not possible, except with time. You cannot now realize that you will ever feel better and yet you are sure to be happy again."*

PRESIDENT ABRAHAM LINCOLN

When the war came to its bloody conclusion in April 1865, the Southern cities lay in ruins, the economy was shattered, and thousands of soldiers began returning home to find their properties destroyed and their families dead from disease or war. Armed bands roamed the countryside, and few saw any hope in the future. Fortunately, President Lincoln was well aware of the devastation the war had caused; he began the conflict for sound political reasons, but it grew into a national horror that he could never have imagined.

When Lee surrendered his army at Appomattox Court House on April 9, for all effective purposes, the fighting came to an end, even though General Johnston's army would remain in the field in North Carolina until April 23 and isolated Confederate units beyond the Mississippi would continue the fight into May.

President Lincoln wanted to avoid any widespread retribution, hoping to reunite the country through a policy of fairness and forgiveness rather than by repression.

*Left: John Wilkes Booth (1838–1865), the man who assassinated President Lincoln. Some claim that his ghost still haunts the stage of Ford's Theatre, where he fired the fatal shot. There's always a method actor hanging around.*

*Left: Abraham Lincoln (1809–1865), the sixteenth president of the United States, portrayed as he gives the Gettysburg Address in November 1863. His assassination ended any chance of quick reconciliation after the war.*

*Right: John Wilkes Booth being tempted by the devil, from a contemporary portrayal of the actor turned assassin. Booth made no less than thirteen appearances in plays at Washington's Ford's Theatre before he returned to assassinate the president.*

One Southerner who was embittered by the war was John Wilkes Booth (1838–1865), brother of the popular tragic actor Edward Booth and a middlingly successful actor in his own right. Booth had served the Confederate government as an agent during the War, operating mainly in Washington and Maryland. When it became clear that the Confederacy had collapsed, Booth decided to take his revenge on the man he deemed responsible. On the night of Good Friday, April 14, President Lincoln attended a performance of the comedy *Our American Cousin* at Ford's Theatre, accompanied by his wife Mary. His wife had almost not gone that night. After an early dinner, Mary complained of a headache and considered not attending the play, but she relented when her husband claimed he would go with or without her. General Grant and his wife had also planned to attend but canceled their plans at the last minute.

Before going to the theater, Lincoln visited the War Department's offices to see if there was any news from North Carolina, where Johnston's army was still at large. He then returned to the White House to pick up Mary and his guests, Major Henry Rathbone and his fiancée, Clara Harris, and the party continued on to Ford's Theatre. The play had already begun when they arrived, so they hurriedly took their seats in the State Box. The door to the box was closed behind them but left unlocked, while a police officer stood watch outside. Lincoln had already dismissed his personal bodyguard, William Crook, so apart from the police officer, the president

was entirely unprotected. Between the second and third acts of the play, the officer, John Parker, left his post and went across the street from the theater for a quick drink. This was the moment John Wilkes Booth had been waiting for. He had been planning an assassination attempt for some weeks, and that morning the newspaper printed a report that both the President and General Grant planned to attend that evening's performance. He had been keeping a watch on the corridor outside the State Box, and shortly after Parker left, Booth made his move. At 10:13 p.m., he quietly opened the door of the box. Both couples were engrossed in the play, and no one saw the door open behind them. Abraham and Mary Lincoln were sitting close to each other, holding hands. Booth raised his small derringer, aimed it at the back of the president's head, and pulled the trigger. Lincoln slumped over the rail, and his wife began to scream. Booth dropped the pistol and pulled out a dagger as Major Rathbone lunged at him. The assassin slashed at Rathbone with his knife, cutting the

soldier's arm. He then leapt from the State Box onto the stage, scattering the leading lady Laura Keene and her fellow actors in the process. When he jumped, Booth caught his heel in the bunting draped beneath the lip of the State Box and landed badly, breaking his left shinbone in the fall. Booth struggled to his feet and yelled out "Sic Semper Tyrannis" ("So end all tyrants") as a last theatrical gesture to the stunned crowd. Suddenly, the theater was in an uproar and became a sea of shouting, screaming, and panic. Somehow, the limping Booth managed to make his escape in the confusion.

However, the assassins hadn't finished their work. Other prominent men were also targets, including Secretary of State Seward. Neither he, nor Grant, another planned target, attended the play. The conspirator marked to murder Grant did nothing; similarly, conspirator George Atzerot was supposed to kill Vice President Andrew Johnson but did not act. (In the midmorning of the next day, Johnson would be swearing the Oath of Office at his Kirkwood House.) Another would-be assassin, however, Lewis Paine, slashed Seward in his home with a knife; despite seriously wounding the politician, he failed to kill his victim.

Meanwhile, several people rushed to Lincoln's aid, the first on the scene being two doctors, Charles Leale and Charles Taft. Accompanied by a nearly hysterical Mary, the party carried the wounded President from the theater, and a government clerk, Henry Safford, offered them the use of his rooms in the Petersen house across the street. Lincoln was laid on Safford's bed, then more physi-

cians were called. The doctors did what they could to save the President. It was hopeless. The bullet had entered the president's skull behind his left ear and had inflicted a mortal wound. At 7:22 a.m., the doctors finally pronounced Lincoln dead. As Andrew Johnson assumed the presidency, the search began in earnest for Booth and his accomplices.

Meanwhile, Booth managed to flee the city in the company of fellow conspirator David Herold, and the men took refuge in a farmhouse before continuing on to the Maryland home of Doctor Samuel Mudd. Unaware of the drama that had unfolded, Mudd treated Booth's injuries, thereby allowing him to continue his flight. However, thousands of troops were combing the area for the wounded actor, and late on April 26, he and Herold were tracked down at Garrett's Farm outside Port Royal, Virginia. Although Herold surrendered, Booth held out until a Union sergeant shot him through the slatted walls of the barn the assassin was hiding in. Booth died of his

*Above:* Ford's Theatre on the 500 block of Washington's Tenth Street was the site of President Lincoln's assassination, and the building is still said to be haunted by the ghosts of those who played a part in the murder.

*Right: When the murderer leapt from the president's box onto the stage, he caught his spur in the bunting used to decorate the box. He landed badly, damaging his leg in the process. Despite this, Booth managed to make a get-away from the theater after fleeing backstage.*

wounds two hours later, during the early morning of April 27.

Lincoln's body lay in state for two days in the East Room of the White House before a funeral carriage carried his body to the Capitol, where it would again lie in state. For a full day, the public filed past the coffin, then the body was moved again, this time to the station. A funeral train took the president's coffin back to Lincoln's home town of Springfield, Illinois, after passing through Philadelphia, New York, Rochester, Buffalo, Chicago, and Indianapolis, where more opportunities were presented for the public to show their respects.

President Lincoln was finally buried on May 4, 1865. When the funeral train reached Buffalo, word reached the mourners that earlier that day General Joseph E. Johnston had finally surrendered his army near Durham, North Carolina. The war was officially at an end. As for Booth's accomplices, most were apprehended, tried, and executed, although the true extent of the conspiracy was never fully determined. Booth and his companions had done their cause a terrible disservice. With Lincoln no longer able to ensure a relatively peaceful reintegration of the secessionist states, President Johnson allowed the Republican hard-liners to dictate policy. The South was to be punished for its mistakes, and after Lincoln's death, harsh military governors and civilian "carpetbaggers" ensured that the southerners paid the full price for their "rebellion."

The immediacy of these tragic and somewhat melodramatic events have faded over the years, but they have also produced a healthy legacy of supernatural tales. The overlooked victim in this drama was Mary Todd Lincoln (1818–1882), whose husband of twenty-two years was shot beside her as she held his hand. She was inconsolable during the weeks following her husband's death, and from then until her death, the assassination dominated her life. She had already suffered a severe blow when her son Willie died in February 1862, and a carriage accident in July 1863 left her with a head injury that caused some concern to her doctors. It was said she was never the same, and during the following year, she held regular séances in the White House in an attempt to reach out to her two dead sons. Her extreme grief following her husband's death never really ended, despite all the best efforts of her two remaining sons. In 1868, she took her youngest son Thomas on an extended trip to Europe, staying in Germany and Scotland

*Left: When Matthew Brady photographed the State Box at Ford's Theater a few weeks after Lincoln's assassination, he captured the ghostly image of a figure standing in the shadows at the back of the box. Was it the ghost of John Wilkes Booth?*

before returning home in 1871. It was there that Thomas took ill and died, the third of her sons to perish through illness.

While her mental health seemed to have been failing since 1863, this tipped her over the edge into insanity. In 1875, her remaining son Robert called a judicial hearing where medical evidence concerning his mother's sanity was given. The hearing resulted in her being officially deemed insane, and as a result, she was forcibly sent to a private mental asylum in Batavia, Illinois. On hearing the court judgment, it is claimed she tried to commit suicide, but the evidence seems to have been suppressed. She remained in the institution for almost a year, before being released into the care of her sister Elizabeth, who still lived in Springfield. Ironically, Mary's new home was the house she had been married in thirty-four years

earlier. A second hearing was called, and this time the decision of the earlier court was reversed. Mary was free to do as she wished, although the rancor between her and her remaining son continued until her death. Fearing another attempt to declare her mentally unfit, Mary returned to Europe, this time to France, where she remained until 1880. On her return to Springfield, her health declined rapidly until July 1882, when it seems she had a stroke. She died the following day and was duly buried beside her cherished husband and her three dead sons.

It was inevitable that supernatural tales soon began to circulate concerning the somewhat tragic figure of Mary Todd Lincoln and of her presidential husband. The most widely known ghost story relating the Lincolns concerns the Lincoln Bedroom in the White House. It was there that their son Willie died

*Right:* *The scene just before the assassination, as reconstructed by eye witnesses. The portrait of George Washington, flags, and bunting distinguish the box used by President Lincoln and his party. The hurried jottings by the sketch artist remind him to "correct the perspective."*

in 1862, although during that time, the room was normally used as a private office for the president rather than as a bedroom. In fact, there is no record that he ever slept in the room. It was there that he signed the Emancipation Proclamation in January 1863. Several occupants of the White House have experienced something unusual in the room. Theodore Roosevelt claimed he detected Lincoln's presence in the room, as did Dwight D. Eisenhower.

The daughter of Ronald Reagan experienced a ghostly presence, while the family dog refused to enter the bedroom. The ghost of the president has even been seen sitting on the bed in the Lincoln Bedroom, pulling on his boots. The account of this sighting came from the highly reputable source of First Lady Eleanor Roosevelt. She screamed and fled from the room, never to set foot in it again. Grace Coolidge was the first person to ever report seeing Lincoln's ghost, staring out of an Oval Office window. President Harry Truman also heard someone

knocking at the door one night but declined to answer. At the time, his daughter Margaret had told him she had felt Lincoln's presence in the hallway outside the bedroom and had heard the sound of knocking or thumping. The president was probably right to be cautious, although the ghost of Lincoln appears to be benevolent. Queen Beatrix of the Netherlands is reputed to have spent a night in the Lincoln Bedroom and was woken by the sound of knocking. When she answered the door, she claims she encountered the ghost of Lincoln, who looked at her and then walked away, as if he had been expecting to see someone else, presumably his wife.

The ghost of Willie Lincoln has also been reported in a second-floor bedroom speaking to members of General McClellan's staff, sharing the floor with the ghost of a British soldier from the War of 1812. This is a little surprising, as the British burned the White House to the ground in 1814; the current building wasn't built until after the war.

Of course, the White House has more than its fair share of alleged ghosts, including Abigail Adams in the East Room, both Abraham Lincoln and Abigail Adams in the second-floor corridors, and Dolley Madison in the Rose Garden. Several White House staff members have also encountered some form of ghostly presence in the Lincoln Bedroom, and almost always this has been attributed to President Lincoln himself rather than to his wife Mary. We don't know where Mary Lincoln used to hold her séances, but she was convinced she could communicate with the dead. In October 1863, she told her half-sister that "Willie lives! He comes to me every night and stands at the foot of the bed with the same sweet adorable smile he always has had. He does not always come alone. Little Eddie is sometimes with him, and twice he has come with our brother, Alex."

Interestingly, she also claimed to have encountered the ghosts of Thomas Jefferson and John Tyler during these séances. Mary clearly believed in spiritualism. After the assassination of her husband, she called in other spiritualists, and according to her biographer, she even attended séances under an assumed name to test the accuracy of the spiritualists' work. She later claimed that during one or more of these sessions, her husband appeared before her.

This propensity to believe in spiritualism also left her open to unscrupulous people. Photographer William Mumler claimed he could capture the "essence" of the dead by photographing the living, and she duly agreed to be photographed by him. When the photograph was released by the photographer, it showed Mary sitting upright with her arm clasped in front of her, while the ghostly image of her dead husband could be seen standing behind her with his arms on her shoulders. He appeared to be gazing down at her with love. Although the photograph was later proved to be a fake, it still seemed to comfort the Lincoln widow in her sorrow. She died a lonely and mentally anguished woman, and it is little wonder that her ghost is still said to haunt the graveside of her family and to appear from time to time in Ford's Theatre. The only one of her children to be buried elsewhere was Robert, who died in 1926 and was interred in Arlington National Cemetery. Strangely enough, he claimed that after his mother's death, Mary haunted him, exacting revenge on his attempt to have her institutionalized. During this period, Mary called her son a "wicked monster" and broke off all ties.

As if this wasn't enough for him, Robert Lincoln also believed he was a harbinger of death. In 1865, he was a twenty-two-year-

*Right:* *President Theodore "Teddy" Roosevelt (1858–1919), the twenty-sixth president of the United States, was one of many occupants of the White House who supposedly encountered the ghost of President Lincoln. Roosevelt also claimed to have encountered a creature not unlike "Old Green Eyes" while hunting in the woods of the Midwest.*

old captain in the army but had returned from his post on Grant's staff to join his father after Lee's surrender at Appomattox Court House. He watched his father and mother leave the White House for Ford's Theatre, then spent the night at his dying father's bedside. After the funeral, he took his mother to Chicago, a city that would remain his home for most of his life. He became a lawyer, married, and tried to have his mother committed during the years that followed, but his nightmare of 1865 returned with a vengeance in 1881. In that year, he accepted President James Garfield's appointment as Secretary of War, and he was in the presidential party on September 19 when the assassin Charles Guiteau gunned down Garfield as he boarded a train in Washington's Baltimore & Potomac Railroad Station. Two decades later, President William McKinley invited Robert Lincoln to join him in Buffalo, New York, where the president was scheduled to visit the Pan-American Exposition. On September 6, Robert Lincoln accompanied

the president on a trip to the Niagara Falls, then later traveled into Buffalo to join him at an evening reception held in the Exposition Music Building. As President McKinley greeted his guests, Leon Czolgosz pulled out a gun and shot him at point-blank range. The president died a week later. Poor Robert Lincoln arrived from the station within minutes of the shooting. He had now been in the vicinity of two presidential assassinations in addition to being present at his father's bedside after his assassination. The man most fervently believed he carried a curse with him, one he blamed on his mother. Needless to say, he never accepted any further presidential invitations.

Others associated with the story also suffered in the years that followed the assassination. William A. Petersen, the tailor in whose house the president died, committed suicide by taking an overdose of laudanum. His body was found in the grounds of the Smithsonian in June 1871. Henry Rathbone and his fiancée, Clara Harris, who shared the State Box with the Lincolns that fateful night, were married two years later and had three children. Rathbone suffered from "dyspepsia" and severe mood swings. He was probably taking an opiate that could be purchased over the counter in the nineteenth century. In December 1883, Rathbone lost his mind. He killed his wife and tried to kill his three children before stabbing himself. He survived, was returned to his native Germany, then held in a German asylum for the criminally insane until his death in 1911.

In February 1869, President Johnson

released John Wilkes Booth's body to his family. They discovered that the head was detached from the body. Apparently, it had been used as grisly proof that the murderer had been apprehended. Several of his vertebrae were also missing and are now in the collection of the National Museum of Health and Medicine. The man who shot him, Sergeant Boston Corbett, suddenly seemed to lose all reason during a meeting of the Kansas State Legislature in 1887. He was restrained, then, like Mary Todd Lincoln, he was declared insane and sent to an asylum in Topeka, Kansas. He escaped the following year, but his subsequent fate is unknown.

If the spirit of Mary Todd Lincoln still haunted the grave of her husband and nursed a wrathful curse on the son who rejected her, her spirit is also reputed to have haunted the place where her husband was shot. Ford's Theatre was closed down after the shooting and remained closed for no less than 103 years. It was only two years old in 1865, but any attempt to reopen it after the assassination led to widespread outcry and even the threat of arson. The following year

it was sold to the government, who used the theater as a repository for army records. The building fell into disrepair, and in June 1893 part of the upper floor collapsed, killing some of the staff who worked in the building. Although it was rehabilitated, the building continued its nontheatrical career, becoming a warehouse and then, in 1933, a museum run by the National Park Service. In 1954, President Dwight D. Eisenhower signed a congressional act to restore the theater.

Reconstruction began ten years later, and a fully restored Ford's Theatre reopened in 1968. By then, the tales of its ghostly associations had become part of the building's attraction. The ghost of Mary Lincoln has been seen in the box, while people who have entered it at night after a performance have sometimes noticed how cold the area was. Others claimed they felt the presence of the ghost of Lincoln, Mary, or both. It was also claimed that footsteps could be heard in the stairs leading to the passageway behind the State Box. Inevitably, these were associated with John Wilkes Booth, reliving his approach to the door of Lincoln's box.

Playing up the notoriety, the theater even produced a play entitled *Mr. Lincoln* in 1980, which appropriately enough followed a run of Dickens's ghost story *A Christmas Carol* set to music. The ghostly musical proved so popular that it has been a regular feature at Ford's ever since.

Photographer Matthew Brady was allowed into the theater in the weeks following Lincoln's assassination, and he took a photo of the scene, encompassing both the State Box and the stage almost immediately underneath it. In the photograph, he claims to have seen the ghostly image of a figure standing in the shadows in the back of the State Box. The photographer claimed it was the ghost of John Wilkes Booth, and Brady remained convinced Ford's Theatre was haunted despite widespread public ridicule of his ghost photograph. It seems as if the ghost of the assassin might still haunt the scene of his crime, although officially the theater staff appears equally convinced that no such ghosts exist. Like so many of these things, it is easy to believe what you want to and to disregard what you don't.

Booth's fellow conspirators were arrested soon after the murder, and his companion David Herold and the other named accomplices George Atzerodt, Lewis Powell, and Mary Surratt were all tried and on June 30, were found guilty of being party to the murder. All were sentenced to death by hanging. Three others whom the authorities claim were party to the conspiracy received life sentences. These men included the unfortunate Doctor Samuel Mudd, whose only crime might well have been being offering his medical skills to the wrong patient. One other conspirator, Edmund Spangler, was given a term of six years of hard labor. His crime had been holding Booth's horse during the assassination, the period equivalent of the getaway driver. Mary Surratt and the three men were hanged on July 7, 1865. Right up until the end, Mrs. Surratt protested her innocence. One of the remaining men died in prison, and Mudd was released following the work he did during a yellow fever outbreak at his remote prison in Fort Jefferson, off the Florida Keys. In 1869, President Andrew Johnson pardoned the surviving conspirators. However, that wasn't quite the end of their story.

The ghost of Mary Surratt seems to have been reported in several places in the years since her execution. Her ghost is still said to haunt the grounds of the Washington State Prison where she was imprisoned and executed, a site that was later turned into a fortification. A boxwood tree is said to keep sprouting on the site of the scaffold, then dying away, something that has been attributed to Mary Surratt as a means of drawing attention to her wrongful execution. Chains have been heard rattling in the rooms in which she and her companions were imprisoned, while the ghost of a sad-looking, middle-aged woman dressed in black has reportedly been seen walking the halls of the fort. Others claim they have been touched by something and felt the presence of a female ghost. Could this be the restless spirit of Mary Surratt? If it is, her spirit is a busy one, as it is also said to haunt

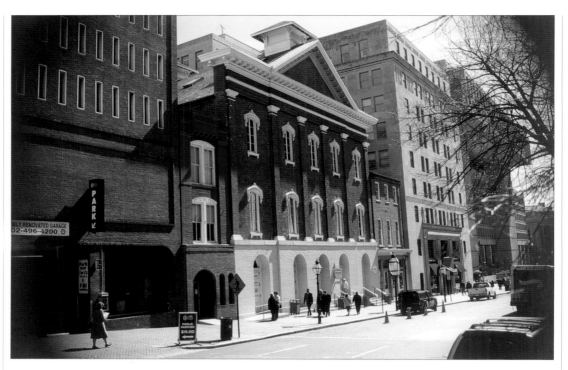

the site of her boarding house at 604 H Street NW in Washington, D.C., as well as the grounds of her home in Clinton, Maryland. The historical Surratt House on Brandywine Road has apparently been the venue for the apparition of ghostly figures in Civil War era civilian clothing, while the ghostly cries of children and the sounds of pacing footsteps have also been reported. As for her boarding house on H Street, it was here that the authorities came to arrest her after the assassination, a home she shared with her son John, who acted as an undercover Confederate courier during the war and frequently played host to John Wilkes Booth. After the property was sold by Mary's daughter Anne, a string of subsequent owners reported hearing the sound of voices, even though nobody has been there, and the sound of a woman moaning and crying. Whether these stories were circulated to give the house some potentially valuable notoriety or whether they have any basis in truth remains unclear. If the ghost of Mary Surratt still lingers, then she seems to divide her spectral time between no less than three haunted venues.

One surprising ghost story associated with the assassination is that of Doctor Samuel Mudd. The involvement of Mudd in the conspiracy has never been properly determined, although at the time there seemed little doubt, since the newspapers vilified him. The public needed scapegoats, so literally, "his name was Mudd." While he was a known Confederate sympathizer and he almost certainly had dealings with the assassin before the murder, his association afterward was probably limited to aiding a wounded man. When Mudd was released four years later, he returned to the Mudd Farm near Bryantown, Maryland, and resumed his practice, where he remained until his death of pneumonia in 1883.

His ghost is still said to haunt his old home. Footsteps have been heard, as have knockings at the door, but in every case nobody was there. The descendants of Doctor Mudd have also seen him around the house, dressed in a waistcoat and shirt, with his sleeves rolled up, as if ready to treat the sick or perhaps preparing to set the leg of Lincoln's murderer.

*Right: The Alabama-born Confederate veteran Lewis Paine was one of Booth's coconspirators, and while Booth was killing Lincoln, Paine attacked Secretary of State William Seward in his home. Seward survived the attack, and Paine was later captured, tried, and executed. It is claimed that his ghost still haunts the site of the Old Club House where Seward lived, even though the property was subsequently demolished. The site is now occupied by the U.S. Court of Claims building, and Paine's ghost has reportedly been seen in nearby Lafayette Park.*

Finally, there remains the ghost of President Lincoln's funeral train, the "Lincoln Special." Pulled by a an engine called the *Nashville*, the train left Washington at eight on the morning of April 21, 1865, and began its winding, 1,654-mile journey through the Union heartland. It also largely retraced the route the President-elect took on his way to take office in 1861, although a detour to Chicago was deemed appropriate due to popular demand. An imposing parlor carriage called *The United States* had been specially designed for presidential use, but this was the first and only time it saw service, the second from last car on the train, followed by a guard's van. The other seven cars in front of the parlor of rest provided carriage space for the twenty-nine Veteran Reserve Corps members of the President's Honor Guard, the president's son Robert, and some three hundred important mourners. Mary Todd Lincoln was too distraught to make the journey. The engine and carriages had been cleaned until the brass on them sparkled, a portrait of Lincoln surrounded by a large wreath was hung in front of the engine over the cowcatcher, while national flags and black bunting and drapes added to the somber impression. The casket containing the president was raised so it would be visible to onlookers as the train passed by at a stately twenty miles per hour. Hidden from sight in the same carriage was the coffin of eleven-year-old Willie Lincoln, whose body had been exhumed so it could eventually rest beside the body of his father.

The tolling of a funeral bell marked the progress of the train, and thousands lined the route to pay their respects. The first halt was in Baltimore, where a grieving Robert

Lincoln felt unable to complete the melancholy journey. He made his own way to Springfield. In Jersey City, the coffin was temporarily removed from the train and borne to City Hall, where upwards of 500,000 people paid their respects.

Back on board, the train and the president's casket continued its journey up the Hudson Valley to Albany, then on to Buffalo, Chicago, and eventually to Springfield. For this final leg of the journey, the *Nashville* was replaced by a brand-new engine called *The Union*. On the morning of May 3, the Lincoln Special pulled into the Chicago and Alton rail depot. Thousands more filed past

the coffin in the State House of Representatives that day, and the following morning President Lincoln and his son Willie were buried in the Oak Ridge Cemetery of their home town. The funeral train had been seen by hundreds of thousands of people during its twelve-day journey.

Many others have continued to watch the train passing along the same route ever since. The ghostly "Lincoln Special" is still said to travel in state on the anniversary of its first passage. In places where the track has moved, it continues along the old route, irrespective of what now lies in the way. Farmers have claimed the train has run through their wheat

*Above: The execution of the Lincoln conspirators took place on June 30, 1865, inside the walls of Old Capitol Prison. The executioner cut up the nooses and sawed the gallows into foot-long pieces as souvenirs. The ghost of Mary Surratt is still said to haunt the site of her execution, which is now part of Fort Lesley J. McNair, a modern military base.*

fields, following the old track, but most refuse to go near the route during late April. Railroad workers in Maryland, Pennsylvania, New Jersey, New York, Ohio, Indiana, and Illinois all have stories of the phantom train. It always seems to appear at night, and in most reports the train appears to be moving silently. Some claim they have seen a band playing some kind of funeral march, but no music could be heard. Most of these sightings have taken place in either New York or Pennsylvania, but the train has also been seen in places all along the route taken by the original "Lincoln Special." Could all of these witnesses have imagined what they saw? Many claimed they were unfamiliar with the story of the train until their ghostly experience, while those more familiar with the story such as railroad workers tend to avoid discussing the subject and certainly have no wish to see the train for themselves.

In her account of the story, the North Carolina writer Nancy Roberts quoted a passage from a newspaper from Albany, New York, which ran:

On the right-of-way of the New York Central, sandhouse men, section hands and track walkers tell the ghost story of the phantom train. The train is pulled by a brand new engine. Put on at New York, The Union pulled the cars across New York state and on to Springfield, Illinois. Railroad men who have seen the train say:

"Late at night, in the last week of the month of April, the air along the track becomes keen - chill. But on either side it is warm and still. The Union and the eight cars travel noiselessly past. If a real train should go by at the same time, the noise of the real train hushes as if the phantom train is rolling over it or replacing it in time or space. As the phantom train passes clocks and watches stop."

As ghostly sightings go, the Lincoln Special surely ranks as one of the most bizarre. In almost every supernatural case, a vision of something is linked to a human being and to a particular event or place. This ghost seems to involve not just people but also a whole train, complete with all the decoration it carried during its journey. Like a ghost ship, it seems doomed to repeat its passage in perpetuity.

It has been argued that the overwhelming collective sense of grief displayed by over a million mourners who saw the coffin make its final journey created such a powerful spiritual energy that the train absorbed some of this, turning it into a supernatural entity in its own right. Others claim that it takes advantage of a rift in time, where the trauma of the train's passing opened a gap that continued to open every year at the same time. Then again, there are others who say the whole thing is utter hokum. What can be verified is that the funeral carriage The United States was destroyed by an accidental fire in an Illinois rail siding back in 1911. That means that if anyone sees the same car passing on the railroad anywhere between Washington, New York, and Springfield, then what they are seeing is truly the ghostly apparition of the Lincoln Special.

# President Davis's Ghost

*"If the Confederacy falls, there should be written on its tombstone: 'Died of a theory.'"*

JEFFERSON DAVIS, 1864

When the first states seceded from the Union in 1861, Kentucky-born Senator Jefferson Davis of Mississippi was elected as the first president of the newly formed Confederate States of America. The fifty-three-year-old had a distinguished military and political career behind him and seemed the ideal man for the job. During the next four years, President Davis ran the Confederacy from his "White House" in Richmond, Virginia, which had become the capital of the fledgling nation. With his military background, Davis was also prone to involving himself in military affairs, much to the annoyance of his commanders. Although he maintained good relations with General Robert E. Lee, Davis was often at loggerheads with his other senior commanders, particularly General Bragg, whom he eventually removed from command. By the summer of 1864, it had become clear that the war was all but lost, with Union armies occupying most of Tennessee, Mississippi, Louisiana, Florida, northern Georgia, and northern Virginia.

His two remaining armies under Johnston and Lee were locked in grinding attritional campaigns around Atlanta and Richmond, and there was no reserve of fresh troops to help these commanders regain the initiative. Through those final days, President Davis remained passionately committed to the Confederate cause and ordered his generals to resist to the bitter end. He encouraged

General Early's small valley army to launch a misjudged attack on Washington, D.C., and he permitted General Hood to launch his ill-fated invasion of Tennessee in the fall of 1864. These were simply the last throes of a desperate man, and by early 1865, with Sherman on the Carolina coast and Grant besieging Lee at Petersburg, it was clear the end was in just a matter of weeks. In March, he sent his family away from Richmond but remained in the city with his ministers. Finally, on April 2, 1865, the Union army finally pierced the defenses of Petersburg, and Lee was forced to abandon the city, escaping to the west with the remainder of his rapidly shrinking army. That afternoon he sent a telegram to Davis: "I advise that all preparation be made for leaving Richmond tonight." The end had come.

That evening, long columns of civilian refugees, soldiers, and government officials fled the city, and at eleven on the night of April 2, President Davis boarded the Danville train and joined the exodus. For the next week Lee led his army west until on April 9, when he found himself trapped by three Union columns near Appomattox Court House, Virginia, and surrendered his army to General Grant. This left Davis and his senior ministers with no army to protect them and with enemy troops scouring the country for them. Within a week, Danville had to be abandoned, so Davis headed south, evading

*Left: Jefferson Davis (1808–1889), the first and only president of the Confederate States of America. Following the war, he was imprisoned in Fort Monroe for two years before being allowed to retire to Beauvoir Plantation, near Biloxi, Mississippi. Upon his death, he was buried with full honors in New Orleans, but his coffin was subsequently taken to Richmond, where his body now lies. His ghost is said to haunt both Fort Monroe and Beauvoir.*

*Right: A portrayal of President Davis from* Harper's Weekly *in 1861, "reaping the harvest" caused by secession. In terms of the carnage that was to follow in the next four years it is a prophetic image; though heaping the blame for the entire War on one man's shoulders cannot be just or accurate.*

*Above: Richmond after the surrender of the Confederate capital. The city has been associated with several ghosts dating from the traumas of the Civil War.*

enemy patrols to reach Greensboro, North Carolina. There he met General Johnston, who commanded the only Confederate army left in the field, where he was told that with General Sherman on his heels, Johnston's surrender of the remaining army was unavoidable. Four days later, on April 17, Johnston surrendered his army near Durham. At Charlotte, North Carolina, Davis learned of Lincoln's assassination. He realized that the Republican hard-liners would view him as nothing but a traitor. He continued south, until May 10, when he was overtaken by a Union cavalry column outside Irwinsville, Georgia. The Confederate president was now a prisoner. He was taken to Fort Monroe on the tip of Virginia's Tidewater Peninsula, where he would remain for another two years. Although he was indicted on charges of treason in May 1866, he was never brought to trial, and a year later he was released on bail. He spent a year touring Europe, and on his return, he was pardoned by President Johnson in a general amnesty.

Davis retired to his home near Biloxi, Mississippi, where he remained until his death in 1889. His remains now lie in Hollywood Cemetery, Richmond.

Today the ghost of President Davis is still said to haunt Fort Monroe, the place he spent two years as a prisoner of the U.S. Government. Fort Monroe was built between 1819 and 1834 as part of a national program of coastal fort construction. It was designed to cover the anchorage of Hampton Roads and the mouth of the James River, and by the time it was completed, it ranked as one of the most impressive fortifications in the country. During the Civil War, it remained in Union hands, providing General McClellan with a base from which to launch his drive on Richmond in the spring of 1862 and giving the U.S. Navy a secure and well-protected anchorage within striking range of Richmond. In 1864, it became the temporary headquarters of General Butler ("The Beast of New Orleans") and his Army of the James. By the time Davis was sent there as a prisoner, Fort Monroe had ceased to be of any real military value but remained a useful bastion in case of any Southern insurrection. Its construction reflected contemporary styles of fortification, with a brick-built central pentagonal casemate or tier of gun embrasures, surrounded by a moat and further protected by the waters of Hampton Roads. On the inside of the casemates, a series of barracks and offices overlooked a central parade ground.

Davis was imprisoned in Casemate 2, where he spent his first few months shackled to the wall. Eventually, when his health deteriorated, his captors relented and removed his fetters, moving him to more healthy quarters elsewhere in the fort. The most commonly encountered ghost story associated with Jefferson Davis is not that of the man him-

*Opposite: When the war ended, Richmond was a shell, with much of the city destroyed by fire. It is said that the ghosts of its Civil War dead still linger in Hollywood Cemetery. In particular, the pyramid monument erected to commemorate the Confederate war dead is visited by the ghosts of numerous fallen soldiers.*

self, but of his wife Varina. She visited him regularly and was concerned about the effect the imprisonment would have on her husband's health. According to the story, her ghost can still be seen inside the fort today, looking out from a second-floor window of the garrison's guest quarters towards the casemate where her husband was imprisoned during his first six months as a prisoner. Indeed, the window is the only one in the fort that directly overlooks the cell where Davis was incarcerated. The room is now a bedroom in the officers' quarters, and occupants of the room have reported seeing the figure of a woman in a long period dress looking out of the bedroom window, while a small girl stands next to her clutching her mother's dress. The figures vanish when they are approached. The window itself has its own peculiar traits, as it is said to occasionally

*Left: Varina Howell Davis, the wife of the Confederate president, visited her husband in prison at Fort Monroe, and her ghost is still said to maintain a vigil in a room overlooking his cell.*

vibrate of its own accord, a movement accompanied by a loud vibrating noise. This phenomenon can last for several hours, usually starting in mid-afternoon and continuing late into the night.

The ghost of Davis himself is also seen, and surprisingly he doesn't usually appear in either of his places of confinement but has been seen walking the ramparts above the casemate, an area he was almost certainly never permitted to go. However, the ghosts of the couple have occasionally been seen in Casemate 2, where Varina appears seated, with Davis on his knees in front of her. The loving wife can be seen cradling the head of her husband on her lap, as if trying to offer him comfort during the darkest days of his imprisonment. The Confederate president and his wife are also said to haunt their home of Beauvoir in Mississippi. It has been claimed that despite the season, certain places in the grounds are noticeably far colder than the surrounding area, and inevitably this has led to conjecture that the cold spots betray the presence of ghosts. Inside the house, the ghost of both Jefferson and Varina Davis have been seen both

*Left: Varina Davis's portrait hangs over a fireplace in Beauvoir Plantation, Mississippi, where the former Confederate President retired to write his memoirs following his release. The couple is still said to haunt the house where they spent their last years.*

FORT MONROE, OLD POINT COMFORT AND HYGEIA HOTEL, V.ª

*Above: Fort Monroe is said to be home to several ghosts. In addition to Jefferson Davis, the ghost of a Native American chief, a Union soldier, and a murdered wife all haunt its walls.*

together and separately, while other ghosts are said to haunt the grounds. After Davis died, the house became a retirement home for Confederate veterans. The ghosts in the garden have been described as old Confederate soldiers, so perhaps the spirits of these battle-hardened old men still linger in the grounds of the house once owned by their Commander-in-Chief.

Jefferson and Varina Davis are not the only ghosts or strange creatures said to haunt Fort Monroe. For a start, the moat is said to contain a sea monster, a little like the legendary Loch Ness Monster in Scotland. While this story strays beyond the realms of credibility, other ghostly contemporaries of President Davis have actually been seen by serving soldiers and their families. The ghost of President Lincoln is said to haunt a partic-

ular room in the same officers' quarters where the ghost of Varina Davis has been seen. Lincoln is usually seen hunched over a desk, as if concentrating on reading a report. General Grant has also been spotted in the same block, as has the ghost of the Native American resistance leader Chief Black Sparrow Hawk, who was imprisoned in the fort during the 1830s. The ghost of Edgar Allan Poe has also been linked to the fort, and like Lincoln his spirit seems to be concentrating on a manuscript in front of him. The writer once served in the fort's garrison and even wrote a short story there, "The Cask of Amontillado," which concerned the ghost of a soldier who was buried alive inside the walls of an old building. However, apart from Jefferson and Varina Davis, the most famous ghost associated with Fort

*Left: The writer Edgar Allen Poe (1809–1849) once served as a soldier at Fort Monroe and wrote one of his short stories there, "The Cask of Amontillado." Appropriately enough, the gruesome tale concerned a young soldier who was buried alive.*

time one that has a strong aversion to roses. It is claimed that in one of the officers' houses on the street, if anyone places a vase of roses in the house, the following morning the petals are discovered on the floor, having been pulled off during the night. Finally, the

Monroe is the "Woman in White." During the 1850s, an artillery captain stationed at the fort, Wilhem Kirtz, was married to a beauty half his age. While her husband was away in Richmond on army business, his wife Camille had a tryst with another far younger French officer. The elderly captain returned to discover the young couple in bed together. Kirtz drew his pistol and tried to shoot the younger officer but hit his wife instead, and she died with the name of her French lover on her lips. While this melodramatic tale appears to have no basis in fact, it does appear that a Captain Kirtz was indeed stationed at Fort Monroe during the 1870s, and an incident during his residency might well have provided the basis for the fort's most enduring ghost story. The ghost of Camille Kirtz is said to haunt the building known as Old Quarters No. 1 as well as an adjacent street within the fort complex that has been nicknamed "Ghost Alley." These officers' quarters seem to be the most haunted area of the fort. She seems to share her haunting patch with another ghost, this

fort is said to be haunted by the ghost of a small child who inhabits the basement of another house occupied by servicemen and their families. The toddler can sometimes be heard laughing and playing with its toys.

*Above:* President Davis spent two years imprisoned in Fort Monroe, during which time he faced a "show trial" and possible execution as a traitor. He was eventually released on bail, although his ghost is still said to pace the ramparts above his cell, a place that, ironically, he was never allowed to visit during his period of incarceration.

*Left:* During the Civil War, Fort Monroe remained in Union hands, a useful bastion in Virginia. In this print, fugitive former slaves are drafted into service to improve the defenses of Fort Monroe and its environs during the Peninsular Campaign of 1862.

# Ghosts of Civil War Prisons

*"All enemies who have thrown away their arms [are]
exposed to the inconveniences as well as entitled to the
privileges of a prisoner of war."*

ARTICLE 49, LAWS OF WAR, GENERAL ORDER NO. 100, APRIL 23, 1863

For the men captured by the enemy during the war, conditions in prison camps were so bad that many must have wished they had fallen on the battlefield instead. Conditions were not always so bad. When the war began neither side had given any real thought to the problems involved in housing and feeding prisoners of war, but the large numbers of men falling into enemy hands made the creation of temporary holding pens a priority. At first an informal arrangement of prisoner exchange helped ease the prisoner-of-war problem, and by the spring of 1862 a formal agreement was made by the combatants, where if at all possible prisoners would be exchanged within ten days of capture for an equal number of prisoners held by the other side. Clearly this situation failed to take into account the vast distances involved in the western theater, as well as the rolling advance of the Union armies and fleets in the Mississippi region.

Similarly, a string of Confederate successes in the east led to a large haul of prisoners. This geographical imbalance meant that any prisoner exchange involved the transport of prisoners of war from one theater to the other, while the threat of enemy attack made the establishment of temporary camps near the front line all but impossible, which again meant transportation problems and lengthy delays before an exchange could be arranged.

*Opposite: This statue sculpted by the late William J. Thompson stands in the cemetery at Andersonville National Historic Site, Georgia. Entitled "Prisoners of War" its three figures that represent humanity, suffering, and death, and are symbolic of POWs from all American conflicts.*

*Left: Fort Pinckney in Charleston Harbor was temporarily used as a Confederate prison in 1861, where Union prisoners captured at the Battle of First Manassas were housed. They were later moved to more secure camps inland.*

Put simply, the system fell apart under pressure. In the summer of 1863, the Union army tried paroling prisoners, where they were released if they promised not to raise arms against the Union ever again. As the Confederacy was short of manpower by this stage, released prisoners were returned to the colors regardless of any agreement they had made with their former captors. In April 1864, General Grant banned any further prisoner exchanges or paroles. From that point on, the prison camps in both the north and the south began to fill rapidly. For the Confederates, this happened at the same time as they were losing their ability to feed their armies in the field or transport supplies around a rail network that shrank with every new Union advance. The result was that Union prisoners of war received the barest of rations, and weakened by hunger, the prisoners became increasingly vulnerable to the ravages of disease. In particular, a lack of fruit and vegetables wreaked havoc on the general health of prisoners in Southern camps. In hellholes such as Andersonville, Georgia, thousands of prisoners were penned up in an area with insufficient sanitation and space, where deaths from disease and starvation increased as the war

drew to a close. Union camps were little better, and prison camps like Elmira, New York, soon developed a reputation that was almost as bad as that of Andersonville. Conditions became even worse when Union Secretary of War Edwin Stanton heard of the short rations in Confederate prison camps, and in retaliation he ordered that prisoners in Union camps should have their rations reduced to the same level as their Union counterparts in the South. The poor rations in places like Andersonville were largely due to the breakdown of the Confederate supply network and the general lack of food to go around. The institution of starvation rations in Union-run camps was simply a form of bitter revenge. As a result, prisoners in both Union- and Confederate-run camps died by the thousands. For the survivors, the physical and emotional scars of the horrendous conditions they endured and the suffering they experienced remained with them to their graves.

Given the terrible conditions in camps such as these, it is little wonder that many sites have been linked with the supernatural, the ghosts of long-dead prisoners who still haunt the camps in which they were incarcerated and where they died.

*Above left: Andersonville, or Camp Sumter as it appeared in late 1864. Although conditions were dreadful, part of the problem was a group of the prisoners themselves known as the "Raiders," who dominated their fellow inmates through a policy of bullying and intimidation. The other prisoners eventually turned on them, and six of the ringleaders were subsequently executed—an event portrayed in this engraving.*

*Above: A temporary prison camp set up at Battle Plain Landing, Virginia, to house Confederate prisoners captured during and after the Battle of Spotsylvania Courthouse. Quite clearly, the camp is a ramshackle mess.*

Probably the most notorious prisoner-of-war camp of the war was Andersonville, Georgia. Officially known as Fort Sumter, Andersonville was the largest prison camp in the Confederacy. Built in early 1864 to contain the large number of Union prisoners who until then had been held in or around Richmond, the sixteen-acre site in Georgia was considered a far more secure location, the camp being guarded by two battalions of local infantry, augmented by a cavalry detachment and dogs. Being on the Georgia Southwestern Railroad, it also had better access to regular provisions than Richmond, although precious few supplies were earmarked for the prisoners, since by that stage the Confederacy was hard-pressed to feed its own people. When it was built, it was designed to hold 10,000 prisoners. By the time it opened its gates in the summer of 1864, some 30,000 prisoners of war entered its gates. Many would never leave. In the fourteen months the camp remained in operation, some 13,000 of the total of 45,000 Union prisoners held in the camp died of disease, starvation, malnutrition, exposure to the cold, or even guard brutality. A lack of adequate food supplies and an almost total disregard for the shelter of the prisoners did little to improve life within the camp, and although the first batch of prisoners was able to build shelters from scrap timber, later arrivals were less fortunate and had to live in the open in all weather.

*Above: Confederate prisoner-of-war handicrafts. Boredom was the least of the worries of those prisoners struck down by disease and starvation, so the skilled work displayed here was made by the lucky ones.*

Inadequate sanitation meant that the local water supply soon became polluted, causing even more deaths through disease. Conditions were reputedly exacerbated by the German-born camp deputy commandant, Captain Henry Wirz, who was the only man on either side to be executed for war crimes once the fighting was over. In theory, the camp remained under the control of General Winder, a veteran of Lee's early campaigns. Although a humane man, other duties meant that he left the day-to-day running of the camp to Wirz. After a string of successful escapes, the commandant devised a "deadline," a barrier creating a "no-man's land" inside the stockade walls that further reduced the space available to the prisoners. Any inmate who so much as touched this barrier could be shot on sight. The regime developed by the prisoners themselves seemed equally harsh. A group of prisoners who styled themselves the "Raiders" dominated the rest of the prisoners through fear, extortion, and violence. The effect was to make the already harsh conditions unbearable.

Finally, the rest of the prisoners joined forces with the guards and "arrested" these Raiders. Assisted by the camp authorities they tried and executed the worst offenders and subjected the lesser Raiders to heavy beatings. By the end of 1864, the worst was over, and many of the prisoners were transferred or even released, as the South was unable to feed them and Sherman's troops were only a few days' march away.

When Wirz surrendered the camp to the Union army, Andersonville's remaining prisoners were released, and the site was demolished. Wirz was duly arrested, tried, and executed by firing squad. Although his crimes were probably insufficient to warrant his being branded a war criminal, the appalling conditions in Andersonville demanded a culprit, and Wirz was the man on the spot.

According to local historians, the ghost of Captain Henry Wirz still haunts the grounds, walking along the road leading to the National Historic Site itself. His ghost has also been seen at the Old Brick Capitol Building in Washington, where he was imprisoned and then executed. The building was torn down to make way for the U.S. Supreme Court, but apparently the echoes of Wirz's footsteps can still be heard in the modern building, just as they could be in the original property. Before the Old Brick Capitol was demolished in the 1920s, the sounds of moaning and weeping could be heard within its walls, along with the sounds of cell doors slamming shut. Worst of all, the occasional ear-piercing scream was also heard before being abruptly cut off as if the ghostly victim was being silenced. When the building was demolished, the ghostly noises stopped.

The only ones that remained were the ghostly footsteps attributed to Andersonville's commandant, Henry Wirz.

The former camp now forms the Andersonville National Historic Site, but the ghosts of Wirz's prisoners are still said to haunt its grounds. Visitors have described a mysterious rising fog that covers parts of the site then disappears as quickly as it came. Even more alarming, the heavy stench of rotting flesh can sometimes be detected around the graves in the National Cemetery, even though the bodies of the dead have long been reduced to mere skeletons. No logical explanation has

*Below: Before release, Confederate soldiers were obliged to swear the oath of loyalty to the Union, as in this sketch made in Richmond.*

ever been given for the smell, and the National Park Service is sure that there is no geological or physical problem in their graveyard.

Others have reported hearing the sounds of a mass of men milling around, some of them moaning in hunger or pain as if the overcrowded camp was still inhabited by its long-suffering inmates. The ghost of the Raiders leader Will Collins is also said to haunt the ground beside the six Raider graves where he and his fellow camp bullies were laid to rest. On two occasions, the sound of his voice explaining the motives behind the murder and extortion of his fellow prisoners has been heard, followed by the babbling noise of what has been described as a lynch mob. The sounds reach a crescendo and then fade away again. In both cases, this experience took place on July 11, the anniversary of the day the Raiders were executed by their fellow prisoners.

The whole experience of visiting Andersonville can be somewhat overwhelming, and for some it would take very little for the experience to "come alive" for them in their own imagination. How this can happen to a group of several people at the same time who share the same strange experience is harder to explain away.

The Confederates certainly didn't have a monopoly on hellish prison camps. The Union camp at Elmira, New York, was almost as notorious as Andersonville. An old army camp was fenced in, surrounded by guard towers and provided with a few rows of wooden lean-to shacks and tents. It then became home to upwards of 10,000 Confed-

erate prisoners of war, some 2,500 of whom died in captivity. This gave Elmira the highest death rate of any camp of either side in the Civil War, a real hellhole for the poor soldiers incarcerated. One Confederate prisoner described the experience:

Elmira was nearer Hades than I thought any place could be made by human cruelty. It was a bend of the small river, surrounded by a high board enclosure, with sentinels walking on a platform near the top outside, with a dead line some fifteen or twenty feet on the inside; and if prisoners went near the line, a wound or death was the invariable result. Snow and ice several feet thick covered the place from December 6 [1864] to March 15, 1865. We were in shacks some seventy or eighty feet long, and they were very open, with but one stove to the house. We had bunks three tiers high, with only two men to a bunk, while we were allowed only one blanket to the man. Our quarters were searched every day, and any extra blankets were taken from us. For the least infraction, we were sent to the guardhouse and made to wear a "barrel shirt" or were tied up by the thumbs for hours at a time. There was one Major Beal who, I believe, was the meanest man I ever knew. Our rations were very scant.

The end of the war brought little immediate relief, as many of the prisoners remained incarcerated until August 1865. Although I have been unable to trace any ghost stories related to Elmira, the ghosts of Confederate prisoners of war have been associated with two other Union camps: Johnson's Island in

*Right: The execution of Major Henry Wirz at the Old Capitol Prison in November 1865. The Andersonville commandant was the only person tried and executed for war crimes in the aftermath of the Civil War, accused of having the blood of 13,000 Union POWs on his hands.*

Lake Erie off the Ohio shore and the largest camp of them all, Point Lookout in Maryland. Camp Hoffman, as Lookout Point was officially called, opened its doors in July 1863, just after the Battle of Gettysburg, and remained in operation until June 1865, two months after the war came to an end. It consisted of two enclosures, comprising a total of forty acres, surrounded by a fifteen-foot-high wooden fence and patrolled by guards. Because of its location, it was extremely humid during the summer months and freezing in winter. Some 54,500 Confederate prisoners passed through its gates, although the camp usually housed no more than 20,000 men at a time. When it was built, it had been designed to house no more than 10,000 prisoners. Almost 4,000 prisoners died in captivity there, although it has been argued that the death rate of 8 percent was less than half

that found among the armies in the field during the same period. Lookout Point is now a well-run state park, and although few traces remain of the camp today, a portion of its perimeter has been reconstructed as a historic attraction. It is said that the ghosts of some of the prisoners still roam the site of the camp today. Numerous visitors have experienced strange things there, and staff members are convinced the site remains haunted. The images of shabbily dressed soldiers have appeared in front of people or their cars, then vanished again, as if the modern-day visitor was permitted a brief glimpse back in time. A few attempts have been made to photograph these soldiers, who were presumably the spirits of the camp prisoners, but no concrete evidence has ever been produced to back up these claims. Like so many ghosts reported in similar circumstances, when the film is developed, the ghostly image of the long-dead soldier is nowhere to be seen. As mentioned earlier, the spread of digital cameras now allows an instant image. This will either "lift the lid" on fraudulent claims, or it might just be the tool needed to provide definite proof that the ghosts of these men still haunt Lookout Point.

Some visitors and staff members have reported hearing voices, the sound of hundreds of men talking and moving around, and this phenomenon has apparently also been successfully recorded on audio tape. Were these the ghostly voices of the Civil War prisoners? Does the spirit of these unfortunate men still linger in the place, a lasting legacy of the suffering endured there? Others have heard the sounds of guards patrolling what would have been the perimeter of the camp, while others report seeing strange movement out of the corner of the eye, but when the observer turns there is nothing there. The site has long been regarded by ghost hunters as a particularly "active" one, and it regularly attracts those who want to experience these sensations for themselves.

The problem with this is that the increased expectation by people well-versed in both tales of the supernatural and the site's history can easily lead to perceived experiences being reported, when in fact nothing of the kind took place.

Ghost-story writer Troy Taylor recounts an incident from the 1970s, where a park manager alleges he saw the ghostly figure of a young man outside the window of his resi-

## RULES AND REGULATIONS
### OF THE
## C. S. MILITARY PRISONS.

I. All orders effecting prisoners of war and the general discipline of the entire command, will be issued only by the officer commanding; and orders proceeding from any other source will not be regarded by officers on duty at the prisons.

II. There will be roll-call daily of the prisoners at 7½ A. M., and at 5 P. M., and the officer of the guard must be present at each.

III. No prisoner, whatever his rank, will be allowed to leave the quarters to which he is assigned, under any pretext whatever, without special permission from the officer commanding; nor shall any prisoner be fired upon by a sentinel or other person, except in case of revolt or attempted escape.

IV. No letters, packages, or parcels of any kind, can be passed into the prison or hospital, without first being examined by the officer commanding, or the Surgeon of the post.

V. Prisoners are not allowed to have any communication with persons outside of the prison, and no visitor will be allowed an interview with a prisoner without permission from the Brigadier General commanding the Department of Henrico.

VI. Prisoners are not allowed to converse with the sentinels; nor must they congregate about the windows after dark.

VII. The firing of one gun at night, or two during the day, will be the signal for the immediate assembling of the guard.

VIII. Under no circumstances will the sentinel be allowed to sit down upon post, or to rest their guns on the ground.

IX. At 9 o'clock P. M., the lights throughout the prison, except in the hospital and officers' quarters, must be immediately extinguished; and it shall be the duty of the Officer of the Guard to inspect the prison at that hour, to see that the lights are put out, fire secured, and that everything is quiet.

X. No conversation, intercourse, or trading with the prisoners, in any manner whatever, will be allowed.

XI. The Officer of the Guard must not be absent at any one time from his post for a period exceeding one hour.

XII. The guard off post must remain constantly at the guard-house ready for instant service, and their guns must be kept on the rack.

XIII. Every guard room must be policed each morning by the old guard, and will not be received, by the officer of the new guard unless in good order. Both the officers of the old and new guard will be held responsible for the execution of this order, and also for the safe keeping of all articles left in the guard house.

XIV. These rules and regulations must be read to the new guard every morning before posting the first relief.

(Signed,)

**TH. P. TURNER,**
Major Comd'g.

Approved,
JOHN H. WINDER,
Brig. Gen. Comd'g Dept. Henrico.

dence before the figure vanished, while another staff member on the site encountered the ghost of a woman standing on a stairway. These and other strange occurrences, such as the sound of footsteps and even the sound of snoring, have all emanated from the old lighthouse that once formed the apex of Lookout Point's prison facility. Taylor is a conscientious writer, and his claim that the site may be the most haunted spot in Maryland is not to be taken lightly.

While Lookout Point had a reputation for being cold in winter, the climate of Maryland would have seemed positively balmy compared to that of Johnson's Island. The Ohio shore of Lake Erie experiences a far heavier snowfall than inland parts of the state, and frosts can last well into the spring. Winter temperatures in nearby Sandusky are often less than thirty degrees Fahrenheit, while spells where this drops as low as negative thirty is not unheard of. The winter of 1864–1865 was particularly cold around Lake Erie, so for the southern prisoners held in the camp on Johnson's Island, these conditions must have been unbearable.

The island in Sandusky Bay was chosen as an ideal spot for a prison camp by Lieutenant Colonel William Hoffman, the man whom the camp at Lookout Point was named after. The camp occupied half of the hundred-acre island and was completed in the first few months of 1862. The first shipment of prisoners arrived in April 1862, and the camp would remain in operation throughout the war. For most of that time, it remained a camp for Confederate officers. Although originally designed for 1,000 men, it eventually housed more than 12,000 inmates, making conditions there almost as bad as they were in Camp Lookout or Elmira. The only saving grace was that the island possessed enough supplies of wood for adequate shelters to be constructed, and until 1864, conditions were Spartan but bearable. However, the camp was inefficiently run and poor sanitation remained a problem throughout the camp's life. That was when Secretary of War

Edwin Stanton drastically reduced the rations given to prisoners in retaliation for what he perceived as deliberate ration cutbacks in Confederate camps such as Andersonville. As the threat of starvation loomed, the instances of disease increased, and at least two hundred prisoners died of illness during the winter of 1864–1865. It is probable that many more died but were buried in unmarked graves on the island. The exact death toll in the camp may never be known. The numbers would probably have been greater had the army not transferred many of the camp's prisoners away during the previous fall.

By April 1865, only 2,800 prisoners remained on Johnson's Island, and they were released after swearing an oath of loyalty to the United States. By June, the prison camp had closed down, and today only a small cemetery and a few memorials remain, including one of a Confederate soldier called "The Outlook" that stares out over the waters of the lake toward the freedom of the Canadian shore. There are also those who say that some of the camp's prisoners never left the island. The cemetery was largely forgotten until 1889, when officials from the State of Georgia raised funs to restore the grounds and tend the graves. It is now a tranquil but somewhat deserted spot, and although the island can now be reached by a causeway, it remains off the beaten path. The island attracts a small number of largely local visitors, and the local tradition has it that the ghosts of Confederate prisoners still walk around the island at night and return to the cemetery during the day. They have also been

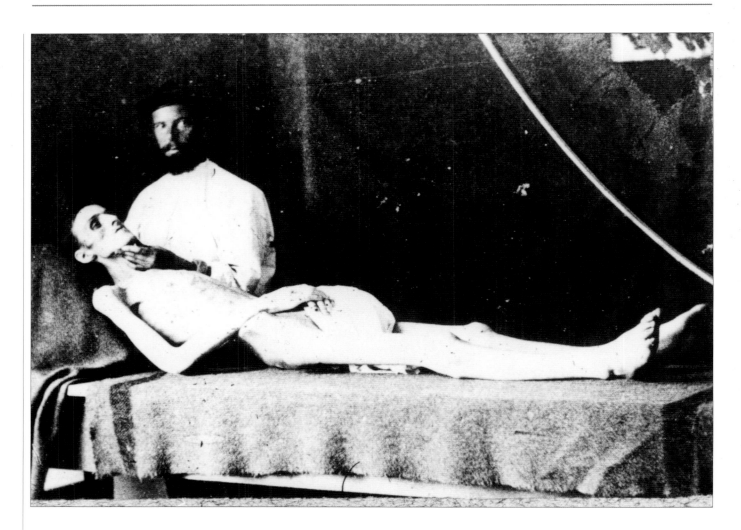

heard but not seen, just like in other haunted prison camps, where the sound of voices and rustling movement, as if from a larger number of immobile people, has supposedly been heard. The North Carolina writer Nancy Roberts went one better, recounting a story that was also told by ghost-story writer Troy Taylor. During the 1950s, a group of Italian workmen were working in a quarry on the island. They must have felt the same about the freezing winters there as did the prisoners from Georgia, Louisiana, and Mississippi that had once shared the same island. The two groups also had one other common bond. Apparently the Italian workmen sang as they hacked away at the rocks in the quarry, and occasionally they heard the sound of other men singing—strange songs the Italians did not know the words to. The men were a little

surprised, but they picked up the tune. This continued over several days, and the tune being hummed changed from time to time. The humming also occurred near sundown, and sometimes it seemed as if the humming came from the mouths of many unseen men. Several of the workmen even saw what they thought were gray shapes standing around them in the quarry, and naturally they assumed the area was haunted.

Several men found excuses to avoid working there anymore, and finally a delegation of the remaining Italians approached their American supervisor. They described the incident to him, but the man seemed reluctant to believe them. He then asked them to hum one of the tunes they heard. The workmen responded with a near-perfect rendition of "Dixie."

*Above: Private John Rose of the 8th Kentucky Volunteer Regiment was imprisoned at Andersonville, and after the camp was liberated, the emaciated soldier was photographed as part of the case against Captain Wirz.*

*Opposite: The Old Capital Prison in Washington, D.C., was a secure military compound used as a transit camp for Confederate prisoners of war, then the prison and site of execution for the Lincoln conspirators and Captain Wirz.*

# Ghosts of the Bereaved

*"There were some who could never be roused any more; grief had stunned and stupefied them forever."*

A VIRGINIA GIRL IN THE CIVIL WAR, *MYRTA LOCKETT AVARY, 1903*

Finally, it is worth mentioning the ghosts associated not with the soldiers who fought in the war or were imprisoned far from home, but those who waited in vain for them to return. One of the most bizarre tales of this kind is set in Carlisle Hall, near Newton, Alabama. This unusual house was built in 1827 by Edwin K. Carlisle, and his descendents still lived in the hall at the time of the Civil War. By that time the house already had a reputation for being haunted; supposedly a blue light could occasionally be seen shining from an upstairs bedroom window, and this was traditionally associated with the late Mr. Carlisle, although a satisfactory explanation for the association or the light has never forthcoming.

His daughter Anne is also said to haunt Carlisle Hall. She was engaged to a wealthy young man from the local area, but when the Civil War began, he marched off to war with other volunteers, serving as an officer in an Alabama regiment. The two planned to wed as soon as he could return home on leave or when the war ended. At the time nobody expected the conflict would last more than a few months, just long enough for the Confederate volunteers to meet the invading Northerners in one climactic battle, then advance on Washington, and end the war in one stroke. Naturally, she was concerned over her fiancé's safety, so to assuage her fears he agreed to send his manservant back to Carlisle Hall with a message after the great battle was fought. They even arranged a code. As he approached the house, the African American servant would carry a white

flag if the fiancé had survived the battle and a red one if he fell in the moment of victory. Anne Carlisle spent the months that followed sitting by a window at the top of the house, waiting for the approach of the manservant. She remained at her post for months, taking meals there and passing the time with friends. Only when it was too dark to see did she return and join the rest of the family in the house. The vigil continued throughout the spring and summer of 1862, until one day in early August she finally saw what she had been waiting for. A horseman was riding up the approach road, and when he came closer she recognized him as her fiancé's manservant. In his hand he clutched a flagpole bearing a small flag.

It was red. Her heart broken, Anne threw herself from the top of the stairs, falling to her death on the floor of the entrance lobby just as the rider came up to the front door. It is said that the house is still haunted by the sound of Anne Carlisle screaming in grief as she relives her last moments, and her ghost can still be seen throwing herself off the top of the long central staircase.

Incidentally, Newton, Alabama is no stranger to ghost stories. Local tradition has it that during the Civil War, a soldier absconded from his regiment to visit his family in the town. He was discovered by the local authorities and summarily executed for desertion by the local Home Guard. Anyone who has read or seen *Cold Mountain* will understand how these militiamen operated. Apparently, he was exceptionally tall, so in order to hang him from the local

*Opposite: The Italianate exterior of Carlisle Hall today. During the Civil War it was the site of a tragic story that led to the alleged haunting of the house by the ghost of Anne Carlisle, whose sweetheart died in the war.*

ALA-765

"hanging tree," the townsfolk had to dig a hole so that his feet wouldn't touch the ground. The story goes that the hole is still there beneath the hanging tree. If anyone tries to fill it in or drop anything in it, by morning the hole is back again, cleaned out and ready for another hanging. Another similar hanging story involves nearby Choc-tawhatchee Bridge, where another wartime execution took place. Again, a hole was dug beneath the tree, because the branch chosen to hang the victim from was too weak and partially broke in midexecution. The feet of the victim were scrabbling in the dirt, so one of the Home Guards who had lost his leg in battle used his crutch to scoop out a hole—with space enough for the victim to dangle and die.

According to tradition, the victim was a Confederate soldier on furlough called William Sketoe. If anyone tries to fill in the hole, the ghost of the hanged man will reappear at night and excavate the hole again. He apparently wanted the proof of his wrongful murder at the hands of the Home Guard to remain visible.

Just to show that Anne Carlisle didn't have a monopoly on grief, it is worth mentioning the tale of Lucy Dabney Smith, the wife of a wealthy tobacco exporter and businessman from Clarksville, Tennessee. In 1858, the newly married couple built a house close to the Cumberland River, a property now known as the Smith-Trahern House, located next to the Riverview Cemetery in Clarksville's McClure Street. Her husband,

*Above: The entrance lobby of Carlisle Hall. According to the story, Anne Carlisle threw herself from the top of the central stairway, and her body lay in this very spot as her sweetheart's servant arrived at the front door, bearing the news of his master's death in battle.*

*Right:* *This bridge crossing the Cumberland River near Nashville, Tennessee, was fortified by Union troops during the war. The establishment of Union control over the Mississippi River and its tributaries allowed men like Christopher Smith to resume trading again.*

Christopher H. Smith, attempted to remain neutral until after the fall of Vicksburg in July 1863. With the Mississippi safe for commerce again, he journeyed down the Cumberland and Mississippi to New Orleans to find a way to regenerate his business. His wife waited for his return, pacing the "widow's walk," an observation balcony on the roof of her home. However, her husband never returned, apparently dying in a river accident on his journey back up the Mississippi. Although she knew she was a widow in mourning, Lucy Dabney Smith still climbed to the widow's walk every day to await the return of her long-lost husband. After the news of his death reached her, she dressed in black, and she would remain in mourning for the rest of her life. She also continued to pace the balcony every day for another three decades, her vigil only ending with her death in 1905. Her remains lie in the town's Greenwood Cemetery.

In the years that followed, the inhabitants of Clarksville or observers on vessels navigating the Cumberland River occasionally saw what looked like a lady in black, standing on the widow's walk of the Smith-Trahern House. Just like Anne Carlisle, Mary Todd Lincoln, Varina Davis, or any of the soldiers, sailors, or statesmen whose ghosts are still said to linger after those tumultuous days, she remains just one more victim of the Civil War.

# Tours, Web Sites & Bibliography

**Ghost Tours**

Ghost Tours of Harpers Ferry
*They also operate the Petersburg Ghost Tours* (see below).
Operates in Harpers Ferry, VA.
Tel. (304) 725-8019 Harpers Ferry, or (804) 733-2401 Petersburg

Ghosts of Gettysburg Candlelit Walking Tours
Operates in Gettysburg, PA
Tel. (717) 337-0445
*An extremely popular and informative tour, based on the Gettysburg ghost observations recorded by ghost-story writer and tour guide Mark V. Nesbitt.*

Farnsworth House Candlelit Ghost Walks
Operates in Gettysburg, PA (Seasonal)
Tel. (717) 337-0445
e-mail: farmhouse@mail.cvn.net
*The original Gettysburg ghost tour, which begins at the Farnsworth House and is operated by its staff.*

Leesburg Ghost Tours
Operates in Leesburg, VA
Tel. (703) 899-4993
http://www.vsra.net/lgt_files/lgtmenu.htm
*Mentions the ghosts of Civil War soldiers at the nearby Drewry's Bluff battlefield.*

The Original Ghosts of Williamsburg Candlelit Tour
They also operate the Ghosts of Yorktown Moonlit Tour.
Operates in Williamsburg, VA (Seasonal)
Tel. (757) 253-1058
http://www.wmbggrouptourservices.com/ghost_public.html
*Includes the ghosts of Civil War soldiers from the Battle of Williamsburg (1862) and the Siege of Yorktown (1862)*

New Orleans Ghost Tours
Operates in New Orleans, LA
Tel. (504) 314-0806
http://www.neworleanstours.net/gandv.htm
*Also runs the New Orleans Haunted History Tour:*
http://www.hauntedhistorytours.com/
Tel. (504) 861-2727

**Web Links**

Ghosts of the Prairie
http://www.prairieghosts.com/
*A superb site for ghost enthusiasts, it is run by the publishers of the ghost hunter's Ghosts of the Prairie magazine and contains a host of useful links. It also maintains a page on the Ghosts of Antietam:*
http://www.prairieghosts.com/antietam.html

Ghost Stories of Harpers Ferry
http://www.harpersferrywv.net/ghost_stories_of_harpers_ferry__.htm
*Contains excerpts from the book* A Ghostly Tour of Harpers Ferry *by Shirley Dougherty, and covers more hauntings than just the ones relating to John Brown.*

Ghosts of Virginia
http://www.vatc.org/pr/feature/SpiritTalesFSO0604.doc
*A catalog of Virginia's ghosts in a document file published as a special feature by the Virginia Tourist Corporation's Public Relations Department. It also contains a useful list of haunted locations, ghost tours, and other relevant information.*

Civil War Ghost Articles
http://www.suite101.com/articles.cfm/civil_war_ghosts
*A useful selection of Civil War ghost stories, including several not discussed here.*

Jonah World
http://wesclark.com/jw/willis_house.html
*A page of fascinating ghost stories, many of which have Civil War associations. It includes excerpts from the book* Ghosts of Fredericksburg *and features the story of the Willis House, while it also covers the ghosts of South Mountain, Maryland.*

Shadowlands
http://theshadowlands.net/
*This rather unusual site has an excellent "places" section, with state-by-state listings of America's most haunted sites. However, to get there you have to wade through references to UFOs, sea monsters, and the abominable snowman. Despite this, the ghost section is pretty comprehensive.*

Bits of Blue & Gray
http://www.bitsofblueandgray.com
*This well-presented web site has a section on Civil War ghosts and strange happenings, and includes a few tales you won't read anywhere else.*

**Bibliography**

Anon; *Guide to Haunted Places in the Civil War* (Columbus, OH, 1996) Blue & Gray Magazine
Bingham, Joan & Riccio, Dolores; *More Haunted Houses* (New York, NY, 1991) Pocket Books
Bochar, Jack & Wasel, Bob; *Haunted Gettysburg: Eye-witness Accounts of the Supernatural* (Gettysburg, PA, 1996) Donny Bayne
Bochar, Jack & Wasel, Bob; *More Haunted Gettysburg* (Gettysburg, PA 1997) Donny Bayne
Coleman, Christopher K.; *Ghosts and Haunts of the Civil War* (Nashville, TN, 1999) Rutledge Press
Garrison, Web; *Civil War Curiosities: Strange Stories, Oddities, Events & Coincidences* (Nashville, TN, 2003) Rutledge Press
Hauk, Dennis William; *Haunted Places, The National Directory: Ghostly Abodes, Sacred Sites, UFO Landings and Other Supernatural Locations* (New York, NY, 2002) Penguin
Hearn, Chester G.; *The Civil War: Virginia* (London, 2005) Salamander
Kermeen, Frances; *Ghostly Encounters: True Stories of America's Haunted Inns and Hotels* (New York, NY, 2002) Warner Books
Kermeen, Frances; *The Myrtles Plantation: The True Story of America's Most Haunted House* (New York, NY, 2005) Warner Books
Konstam, Angus (ed.); *The Civil War: A Visual Encyclopaedia* (London, UK, 2001) PRC Publishing
Konstam, Angus; *The Pocket Book of Civil War Battle Sites from Manassas to Atlanta* (London, UK, 2004) Greenwich Editions

Konstam, Angus; *The Pocket Book of Civil War Weapons, from Small Arms to Siege Artillery* (London, UK, 2004) Greenwich Editions
Norman, Michael & Scott, Beth; *Historic Haunted America* [also published as *Haunted America*] (New York, NY, 1996) Tor Books
Nesbitt, Mark V.; *Ghosts of Gettysburg: Spirits, Apparitions and Haunted Places of the Battlefield* (Gettysburg, PA, 1991) Thomas Publications
Nesbitt, Mark V.; *More Ghosts of Gettysburg: Spirits, Apparitions and Haunted Places of the Battlefield* (Gettysburg, PA, 1992) Thomas Publications
Nesbitt, Mark V.; *Ghosts of Gettysburg III* (Gettysburg, PA, 1995) Thomas Publications
Ramsland, Katherine; *Ghosts: Investigating the Other Side* (New York, NY, 2001) St. Martin's Press
Roberts, Nancy; *Civil War Ghosts and Legends* (New York, NY, 1992) Metro Books
Symonds, Craig L.; *The Battlefield Atlas of the Civil War* (Baltimore, MD, 1983) Nautical & Aviation Publishing
Taylor, L.B. Jr.; *The Ghosts of Fredericksburg* (Richmond, VA, 1991) Virginia Ghosts
Taylor, L.B. Jr.; *Civil War Ghosts of Virginia* (Richmond, VA, 1995) Virginia Ghosts
Taylor, Troy; *Spirits of the Civil War: A Guide to the Ghosts and Hauntings of America's Bloodiest Conflict* (Alton, IL, 1999) Whitechapel Productions Press
Toney, Keith B.; *Battlefield Ghosts* (Charlottesville, VA, 1997) Howell Press
Winer, Richard & Ishmael, Nancy Osborn; *More Haunted Houses* (New York, NY, 1981) Bantam Press

Acknowledgments

Chrysalis Books Group Plc is committed to respecting the intellectual property rights of others. We have therefore taken all reasonable efforts to ensure that the reproduction of all content on these pages is done with the full consent of copyright owners. If you are aware of any unintentional omissions please contact the company directly so that any necessary corrections may be made for future editions.

R = Right  L = Left  C = Center  T = Top  B = Bottom

All images © Chrysalis Image Library apart from the following:

Library of Congress, Prints & Photographs Division 22 (LC-DIG-cwpbh-03576), 25 Civil War Photographs, (LC-DIG-cwpb-01471), 29L HABS, (HABS, DEL,1-DOV,6-1), 29R HABS, ( HABS, DEL,1-DOV,6-4), 30L HABS, (HABS, DC, WASH, 8-20), 30R HABS, (HABS, DC, WASH, 8-53), 31 HABS, (HABS, DC, WASH, 8-27), 32B Civil War Photographs, (LC-DIG-cwpb-03739), 34 (LC-USZC2-2703), 36 (LC-USZ62-115350), 37 Civil War Photographs, (LC-DIG-cwpb-04106), 39 (LC-USZ62-115350), 48 Civil War Photographs, (LC-DIG-cwpb-01127), 49 HABS, (HABS, MD,22-SHARP.V,18-2), 59T (LC-USZ62-100659), 63 HABS, (HABS, PA,1-GET,7-1), 64 (LC-USZC4-1041), 72 Civil War Photographs, (LC-DIG-cwpb-01450), 73 Civil War Photographs, (LC-DIG-cwpb-00888), 76B (LC-USZC4-5796), 82 (LC-USZ62-93015), 82 (LC-USZC4-6702), 83 (LC-USZ62-105075), 89 (LC-USZ62-131082), 92 (LC-USZC4-1910), 100 (LC-USZC4-1756), 109 (LC-USZC2-2807), 124-125 Civil War Photographs, (LC-USZC4-7948), 127 Civil War Photographs, (LC-DIG-cwpb-01280), 135 (LC-USZC4-2540), 136 (LC-USZ62-7040), 145 Civil War Photographs, (LC-DIG-cwpb-03049), 146-147 (LC-USZ62-133068), 147T (LC-USZ62-6-1548), 148 Civil War Photographs, (LC-USZ62-107446), 152T (LC-USZ62-25166), 153 (LC-USZ62-8933), 158 (LC-USZ62-26399), 170T (LC-DIG-ppmsca-07786), 172T (LC-USZ62-10610), 181 Civil War Photographs, (LC-DIG-cwpb-04195), 187 HABS, (HABS, ALA,053-MARI.V,005-93), 188 HABS, (HABS, ALA,053-MARI.V,005-9), 189 Civil War Photographs, (LC-DIG-cwpb-02091).

40L & 131 © TRH/U.S. National Archives
57 © Bettmann/CORBIS
129 © Medford Historical Society Collection/CORBIS
104-105 © Montgomery County Historical Society
119B © Shirley Plantation